MUSIC AS CULTURE

By

Marcia Herndon

And

Norma McLeod

Published by MRI Press, P.O. Box 362, Pt. Richmond, CA 94807

First Edition published in 1979 by Norwood Editions, Darby, PA
Second Edition published in 1981 by Norwood Editions, Darby, PA
ISBN 0-8482-4479-6, lib. bdg. ML3798.H46

Second Edition, paperback, published in 1990 by MRI Press
ISBN 0-9627473-0-0, Second Printing, 1993

10 9 8 7 6 5 4 3 2

Second Edition

CONTENTS

Preface to Second Edition

MUSIC AS CULTURE

We greatly appreciate the opportunity to prepare a revised and updated edition of *Music As Culture*. That this edition should be presented only two years after the initial printing is a source of real pleasure to us, since it allows us to take full advantage of the comments and suggestions of our colleagues. In particular, we should like to thank David P. McAllester, Stephen Feld, and Cynthia Tse Kimberlin, whose generous and thoughtful help has been much appreciated.

We have included those developments in theory, practice and focus which have emerged since the beginning of the first edition. For example, thorough investigation of many questions now tends to demonstrate that music is not subliminal and nonverbal as was once thought. Rather, ethnomusicologists have begun to view it as a consciously manipulated phenomenon. Music is *constructed, discussed*, and *judged*. Innovation takes place as much in the light of social pressure as in that of aesthetic judgment. Thus, while ephemeral, music ranks as one kind of social fact, fully amenable to the manipulations applied to other social facts.

Yet music remains a creative aesthetic act, still representing many unanswerable questions. The heavy patterning and redundancy balance against its innovative creative aspects. Music fits within the society in which it develops, to be sure. Yet each music is an endless source of variation and change, and sometimes transcends its function.

We agree with King (1980) that in watching the interplay of action in a creative art, we feel the need to re-define social structure from that which is normative and patterned, to that which is possible. It is the nature of art to seek the outer limits of itself, and having found them, to move into the unknown. The creative person may represent society part of the time; but sometimes, one blunders beyond the known response -- the standard answer. One is not always the social animal; the creator also represents the seeker and thus confounds all the sage comments concerning traditional forces within human life.

Hopefully, we shall be happily debating these and other facts of music -- the patterned and the creative -- for some time to come.

This edition owes much to the kindness of Norwood Editions, who have believed in us from the beginning. In particular, we thank Jerome Weiman, without whose interest this book could never have been published. We also owe much to Billye Talmadge, who has once more valiantly struggled with our copy and won out over both of us; and to Carmah Scott, whose eagle eye pounced on typos and split infinitives three other proofreaders failed to see.

Norma McLeod

University of Ottawa
June, 1981

Preface to First Edition

MUSIC AS CULTURE

This book is the direct result of extensive discussions, telephone calls and correspondence with many colleagues. At the annual meeting of the Society for Ethnomusicology in 1971, a number of people came together in a casual discussion of the needs of ethnomusicology. A number of areas were identified at that time, with agreement that the immediate need was for a comprehensive textbook for introductory courses in ethnomusicology. Although it was recognized that several good books are available, no one book had, to that point of time, attempted a synthesis of both the cultural and musical aspects of ethnomusicology.

Accordingly, we, the authors, set out to identify the areas which everyone agreed upon as necessary in a comprehensive introductory text on ethnomusicology. Having circulated a questionnaire and elicited responses both formally and informally from a wide range of colleagues, we created an outline. Our main area of concern was with the range of implications which music has, both as a product of human behavior and as an integral part of human interaction.

The first questions which arise in preparing an introduction to ethnomusicology are: "What is music?" and, "What is ethnomusicology?" In answering the first question, although agreement is reached that music is humanly structured sound, its particular aspects vary from culture to culture. The second question is even more difficult to address than the first, since it is necessary to consider approaches to music from anthropology, musicology, folklore, linguistics and, more recently, from a combined perspective of all the preceding.

The key to ethnomusicological investigations is field work in living societies. Field work is not simply a matter of knowing and acquiring equipment, taking recordings and photographs, keeping a journal and knowing procedures. Rather, one must have a firm ethical base and sound ethnographic background in order to prevent the recurrence of such atrocities as Densmore's teaching American Indians how to "sing properly" before she would record them (as mentioned in Sachs, *The Wellsprings of Music*). In addition, one must know how to formulate hypotheses and test them.

In the formulation of hypotheses, it is helpful to consider current theory concerning the musical occasion, the possible contexts for musical performance, and how context may affect musical form. Knowledge of the status and role of musicians and their interrelationships with audiences is important background for the ethnomusicologist; as is knowledge of perception and the learning process (cognition, proximics, myths, evaluation of performance, teaching methods, learning abilities). Music often plays a vital role in rituals, ceremonies, politics and social control. It may also be involved in many other aspects of human life. Since human groups are continually in a process of change, it is necessary to have some idea how music changes with time, and what factors may institute or prevent change from occurring.

Music may be removed from its context and considered as an isolated entity. In so doing, one traditionally transcribes recordings. This process initiates two major types of problems: the nature and goals of transcription and the fallibility of Western notation. It therefore becomes necessary to discuss not only the problems, conventions and aims of transcription, but also how the goals of the ethnomusicologist influence the choice of transcription philosophy. A good example of this is found in England's Symposium on Transcription in *Ethnomusicology*, 1964, in which several scholars transcribed the same piece, with markedly different strategies and results.

Since Western notation is incomplete -- not allowing for indication of such things as upglides to a pitch, rasp, or dozens of other performance devices -- additions and alterations to the traditional notation system must be made. Mechanical aids to transcription should be evaluated. Finally, a methodology for transcription must be included.

Once the problems of transcription and notation have been considered, the real problems of analysis emerge. Ideally, analysis should usually precede transcription. Approaching analysis in terms of its possible goals, each of the following should be considered: size of sample; determination of analytic elements; aesthetics and value systems; variation; definitive performances; analysis of a single song versus analysis of a style, form, or genre; and computer assistance.

Since much of the world's music is sung, it is only natural that attention be given to the relationship between music and language. What are the boundaries of speech and song, and how does one determine them? Does music constrain text, or does text constrain music? Are "nonsense" syllables really nonsense, or might they carry meaning? What are the possible levels at which meaning may reside in music?

If music is a code or a multi-dimensional symbolic system, full clarification and decipherment of the code or symbol systems is vital.

In moving toward an ethnomusicological perspective, knowledge of what the analysis of sound reveals about culture is needed. Also, knowledge of what the analysis of culture reveals about sound is needed. Whatever its particular form may be, the interrelationships of music and culture is real, integral, basic and approachable.

The limits, goals and prospects for ethnomusicology are similar to culture in that they are always changing. Through a view of past ideas and influences, it becomes possible to understand current trends: preoccupation with analysis, utilization of linguistic theories, search for objectivity and understanding.

Ideally, an introductory text should cover all aspects of human musical behavior. The ultimate objective has long been the fusion of the specifically musical and the specifically behavioral aspects of ethnomusicology.

There has been a continuing tendency toward separation between music studies and cultural studies. Unfortunately, Merriam's remarks about "...books, music, which is often treated as an object in itself without reference to the cultural matrix out of which it is produced" (1964:vii-viii) are still here. At the same time, there is an abundance of anthropological, linguistic and folkloristic studies which do not consider the musical parameters.

In short, the wholeness of an emergent discipline which gives equal consideration to the music, itself, and the behavior surrounding its origin, production and evaluation still eludes us.

The original intent of this book was to bridge the chasm separating these two camps. Accordingly, the authors planned, projected and produced a manuscript which would address itself to all aspects of the scholarly investigation of music. However, the anonymous readers who evaluated the manuscript in its totality eventually brought us to the realization that the ideal of a total discipline has not yet been achieved.

It was perfectly clear that two of the evaluators were musicologically inclined, because they indicated distrust and disdain of the behavioral portion of the book. Two other readers were anthropologically inclined, indicating disdain with the musicological portion of the book. One reader understood and applauded both segments equally.

After much discussion and with a great deal of reluctance, it was finally decided that the manuscript would be divided into two parts. It should be made clear, however, that the authors do not feel that any introductory approach or any professional approach to the study of music should exclude any aspect of the investigation of music. We deplore any remaining feelings that a total study of music as culture or music as a fixed item of sound can be totally comprehensive without a full coverage of its so-called complementary aspects. We look forward to the day when such discussions are not only outmoded, but also unthinkable.

In preparing this book, we have drawn upon wide range of examples from various areas of the world. We have not made any attempt to cover all of the geographic areas, or to arrive at a fair sampling of representative examples from the entire world. Instead, the strategy has been to use examples from our own field work which covers everything from urban musics, to peasant musics, to those of hunting and gathering societies.

Primary emphasis throughout the book has been placed on ethnographic material from Malta. In so doing, we have made a conscious choice to provide the student with as much information as possible about a single musical culture. We have done so with the intent of providing a fairly comprehensive view of the various approaches one might take to musical behavior within a single culture. It is expected that the instructor using this book in an introductory course will add his or her own field experience within the lecture framework, thus providing the student with a contrast of information. The result, it is hoped, will be a depth of understanding which can be transformed to whatever situation in which the individual might find him/herself.

Another strategy in the preparation of this book has been to maintain a thoroughly professional stance. Although our full expectation is that most students or other interested readers will never earn a livelihood by professionally studying musical cultures, nevertheless, we feel that the exposure to professionalism will provide a formal insight which will enrich one's appreciation of his/her own music.

Perhaps a more selfish stance is the hope that people who are not themselves musical specialists will have the courage to produce articles, monographs and books dealing with the information they find. Ethnomusicology is a field of study which has few practitioners and vast areas of study, geographically and culturally. Therefore, it becomes necessary to have input from a multitude of sources in order to sufficiently understand the true nature of the diversity of music as human behavior.

In preparation of this manuscript, thanks are due to many, many people. All of those who befriended and helped us in our various field studies are the primary sources of inspiration. All the students who heard the ideas in the formative stages, and the colleagues who have provided various kinds of input are muchly appreciated. In particular, Charlotte Frisbie, Barbara Krader and Robert Garfias are greatly appreciated.

Also, thanks are due to the various organizations which have provided funding for portions of this study: the Wenner Gren Foundation for Anthropology; Tulane University; the University of Texas; the University of California at Berkeley; and the University of Ottawa. The tireless efforts of Linda Moran in typing the first, second and third drafts of the manuscript are truly appreciated. Finally, thanks is due Billye Talmadge who valiantly undertook the massive task of editing this material and preparing it in its final form.

In retrospect, the final appreciation should be for the opportunity afforded by the writing of this manuscript because it has given us a chance to review the field, its current situation, and its future prospects.

Marcia Herndon

Berkeley, California
May, 1979

1

SOUND, MEANING, AND DIVERSITY

Ethnomusicologists study music in different cultural settings, which creates two major questions: "What is music?" and, "What is ethnomusicology?"

The incredible diversity of music throughout the world makes it necessary to consider the first question because, if the term *music* is not clearly defined, then the same hesitancy applies to the sub-discipline or focus represented by the clumsy term *ethnomusicology*. In this introductory section, only the broad implications of these two questions will be discussed.

THE NATURE OF MUSIC

Definitions of basic terms are elusive and, as might be expected, many variations exist in the definitions of music which are readily available.

The *Harvard Dictionary of Music*, a standard reference

source, approaches the definition in a historical manner, citing Greek and Egyptian concepts, and mentioning the sub-categories for music in the Middle Ages (Apel, 1969:548-549). This classificatory approach is a common one, but the authors' information about music rests on its classification within any society. Definitional problems become apparent when a *universal* view is attempted.

Most definitions imply that music is a form of sound and that it is a human activity. Sometimes, music is defined by its subdivisions; sometimes, by its characteristics (pitch, rhythm, intensity, timbre). Occasionally, one finds the term "singing" loosely applied to other creatures, such as whales, or "dancing" applied to the courtship movements of birds. It is generally agreed, however, that music is sound (and sometimes movement); that it is created to be performed and listened to; and that those who participate in it and/or appreciate it are human beings.

Bird cries are a case in point. Are these music or territorial signals? To be music, sound must be fairly lengthy in extent and have variance both within a performance and between performers. With the exception of the imitative birds, such as the mockingbird, these criteria are not met.

Studies of the dolphin indicate that these intriguing sea mammals have a wide range of sounds, which may be something like language. They have been known to try to reproduce human sounds under laboratory conditions as well. Here is one of the elements which might be expected from music: a wide range of sounds, apparently recombined continuously. Until the evidence is complete, it is difficult to tell whether the dolphin is a singing mammal or a speaking mammal. In either case, the exclusiveness of mankind is being broken, but it is presently difficult to determine in which direction the dolphin approaches our sound-making patterns.

The work of Jane Goodall (and others) on chimpanzees in a natural environment also tends to make humanity less an exclusive club. Analyzing the sounds of chimpanzees is now underway -- sounds which include a wide range of coughs, grunts, whoops and pitched sequences. The sequences with pitch are of most interest to music students, of course; it is a great shock to hear chimpanzees "singing" major triads. Until the analysis is complete, it will not be known whether these sounds represent a language, a set of signals, or a very simple music.

The older literature on Africa contains occasional references to dancing among chimpanzees. Until physical anthropologists began a close investigation of primates in their natural habitats, all these accounts had to be disregarded. The dramatic image of chimpanzees flinging mud at a spot on the ground until a central platform was built up; the delightful idea of a group of chimpanzees circling the platform, arms waving, whooping, while one old male beat vigorously on the platform -- such stories were dismissed as fantasy -- until scientists actually saw it occur.

Chimpanzees are among the primates customarily brought to the Delta Primate Center near New Orleans, Louisiana, where they are used for medical and behavioral experiments. The first group imported, which came directly from their natural environments, were not well and were isolated from the other species for treatment and study. This is significant, in that zoo-bred animals are now thought to behave quite differently from free-ranging members of the same species.

At the time of the authors' observation, this group of chimpanzees was restless, sick and angry. They were caged separately in a large square area, with each cage open to the outside world.

One old male was aimlessly playing with a piece of tin which projected from the bottom of his cage. He struck it with his clenched fist and the sat back. A moment later, he struck it again, two or three times. Then he raised his head and gave a series of high barking sounds which were immediately repeated by all the chimpanzees in nearby cages. He returned to the piece of tin and began striking it rhythmically with alternate fists, barking all the while. The other chimpanzees rose in their cages, barked furiously (but not in unison), and raising their arms above their heads, began to skitter about their cages. It was not a regular dance nor were the sounds coordinated in any way, but the old bull gave a steady, continuous beat on his piece of tin.

But was it a dance? Not quite. The restricted animals could not see one another and thus could not coordinate their movements. However, reports from Africa indicate that such activity does occur, mainly in the rainy season. When chimpanzees in a troupe are thoroughly wet from the continuous rains, tempers shorten, and eventually the animals will break into a sort of furious barking, accompanied by much arm-waving and skittering. Reports of the great mud drum have not been verified, however.

Such examples will undoubtedly multiply as more is known about animal behavior. Since man is a primate, it is

4

probable that behavior similar to music occurs among other primates. Some biological base can be assumed for music-making, although at present, the evidence is far too tentative to discuss. This does imply, however, that ethnomusicologists may be recording primates other than man in the not-too-distant future.

Until such time as the evidence is fuller, one can only speculate that man is probably not the exclusive music-maker. Much will depend, however, on how one chooses to define music. Are chimpanzees making music when they bark? Does a regular drumming beat constitute music? Will dance notations be able to record their skitterings and arm-wavings? Will their activity be formal enough to constitute dance and music?

MUSIC AS HUMAN ACTIVITY

Before one can begin to say what constitutes music in the broadest possible sense, one ought to be able to say what, of human activity, is music. This is not easy. As long as music students are dealing with their own music, they are fairly sure of the borders between music and non-music. Any music specialist will say that music should have certain general characteristics, such as pitch and rhythm, and will be able to distinguish between music and non-music at least in his/her own area of concern.

The distinction between music and noise is never an absolute one, but a matter of cultural conditioning, personal idiosyncracies and group identity. What is accepted as music by one group or generation may be ignored or dismissed by another. As a human activity, then, music is culturally defined. For a good illustration of this, one has only to examine the statements quoted in *The Lexicon of Musical Invective* (1965).

In the study of musics outside one's own culture, even greater definitional problems are presented. The Maori *haka* or war-dance is not sung, but shouted rhythmically. Yet, in spite of its lack of pitch, it must be regarded as music because the Maori so regard it. The Cuna Indians make fine distinctions among styles of vocal expression. Instead of separating speaking from singing (and, by implication, language from music), they have three "ways of speaking", at least one of which would be identified by an outsider as singing (Bauman and Scherzer, 1974:263-282). The Koran cannot be sung, since music is not allowed in the Muslim religion. Therefore, reciting the Koran cannot be called music, even though it is pitched.

These few examples give some idea of the difficulty of defining music only in a human sense, without including the behavior of other animals. If a hard line is taken, defining music as a form of sound with certain characteristics, such definition will be forced to exclude numerous examples of sound from consideration. If, on the other hand, the cultural definition of music is followed in each case, some kinds of sound normally thought of as music may be omitted.

LIMITS ON MUSIC

There are certain biological aspects to the study of music, mainly pertaining to the outer limits of perception. The perfect human ear can hear sounds between approximately 20 and 20,000 cycles. The average person of 36 years of age or so can hear only to 8,000 cycles, because hearing loss of high pitches often occurs first. Sounds softer or

6

louder than certain levels are also hard to discern. Ten to 100 decibels is a reasonable range for human hearing; below 10 decibels the sounds may be inaudible; while above 100, they may register as pain rather than sound.

Numerous mechanical devices can produce sounds which are inaudible. The most common is the Jew's Harp, which uses overtones on a single fundamental to produce a melody. When the tuned prong is struck, it sounds a fundamental pitch plus a stressed overtone. The strength of various overtones is altered by changing the shape of the mouth cavity. One overtone is emphasized at the expense of others; these latter are not heard and are not part of the music.

Electronic devices sometimes exceed the limits of human hearing, both in producing and recognizing pitch. The commonest is the signal generator which can produce sounds into the range of microwave. At the upper end, the sounds produced are so slow as to register as clicks rather than pitches. Thus, pitch is a function of the rate of vibration. Another such device is the Melograph, which registers pitch, loudness and timbre.

There are also limits on duration. When a sound is too short, it will not be heard; when too long, it will not be heard as music.

Information about other biological limits on music comes from studies of the brain, where it has been shown that some aspects of music are stored in the sub-dominant cerebral hemisphere, others in the dominant (*Music and the Brain*, 1977).

Although the brain is divided into two symmetrical halves, one side stores speech and is dominant over the other. In the musical specialist, musical information passes over to the dominant side of the brain.

Persons with brain damage only on the speech side of the head may lose the power to speak, but may still be able to sing. Oddly enough, brain-damaged persons of this type frequently retain the words to songs in addition to the melody. From this, it can be assumed that songs with words are stored as a whole, a fact which explains the difficulty some people have in speaking the words of songs without singing them. EEG tracings made of musicogenic epileptics show that attacks from listening to music occur in either the right or left hemisphere, which indicates that both hemispheres are involved in music-learning (op. cit:344-353).

While little is known about the mechanisms involved in the storage of musical information, all ethnomusicologists have encountered one or another of the physiological reactions which occur when listening to music other than one's own.

Each individual with average hearing learns and stores certain kinds of musical information early in life. For example, European children are taught to play "in tune" and pitch perception is high, storing information of an exact nature about pitch. In some cases, pitch learning is so firm that individuals develop "perfect pitch" which is the ability to name or reproduce pitches within very narrow limits. When a trained musician becomes an ethnomusicologist, he or she is forced by the nature of the work to listen to pitch spacings which may vary significantly from his/her own.

Persistent listening to non-Western music pitch sequences for a considerable length of time tends to cause the listener to either accommodate the pitches heard to his/her own system, or not. If accommodation is possible, the listener remains comfortable. If, however, the pitches in question are so different that accommodation is impossible, the listener may suffer some form of physiological discomfort. Migraine headache, diarrhea, stomach cramps, double vision, or extreme muscle tension is common. Once a musical system is well-learned by an individual, one conclusion is that it interferes with new information. This represents a significant contrast with language. Given time and training, almost anyone can learn a second language; to learn a second musical system may be painful, however.

The dominant cerebral hemisphere is involved in this process, as well. If one is given verbal information about pitches in a new music, the listening process is less likely to be physiologically disruptive. This implies that there is some form of transfer of information possible between the cerebral hemispheres, so that verbal information stored in the dominant hemisphere can allow new learning to take place in the sub-dominant. Unless this were so, no person trained in one culture could ever sufficiently learn the music of a foreign culture. As there are many successful examples of new music-learning, this is obviously not the case.

The biological limits on music recognition are perhaps not as significant as the cultural. As mentioned above, duration of sound, if too long, will not be heard as music. This is more prominent when patterns of sound are considered. While precise documentation for types of musical patterns which humans can perceive is not yet available, many cultural factors may be involved. Phrases in Western music generally do not exceed approximately seven seconds. Verses or strophes of phrases are usually fairly short, as well; four to six phrases within a strophe are normal. In Japanese music, however, one can listen to up to fifty sound segments before a sequence is repeated. Thus, human beings can be trained to expect sequences of sound of various lengths, with cultural considerations dictating the length.

This appears to be true also of longer sequences or patterns of music. Western opera usually ranges between fifty minutes for a short opera and five hours, perhaps, for a Wagnerian opera. Japanese or Indian music may continue for much longer periods of time without distress to the audience. Again, this is cultural rather than biological. In the longer performances, Eastern audiences are allowed to move about which is impossible for a Western audience imprisoned in an opera house, waiting for the second act to end. Thus, the nature of music is definable at its boundaries both in terms of biological and cultural limits.

Perhaps even more important than the biological limitations on music are the cultural. Since music is a human activity, it occurs within the context of group activity. Unlike some other species, such as the wombat, humankind always lives in groups, no matter how small. The qualities of group life which are learned and passed from generation to generation as survival factors for the group are collectively called culture by anthropologists.

For the most part, culture is investigated through the normal behavior, verbalizations and symbols of mankind. Anthropologists seek the pattern in human behavior and ignore the unique. As Nadel states:

> The forms of behavior...with which we are primarily concerned are the recurrent, regular, coherent, and predictable. The subject matter of our inquiry is standardized behavior patterns; their integrated totality is *culture* (cf:1951:-29).

Culture, then, is normalized statements about the nature of the behavior of a group of people attempting to live together. Such behavior is standardized by the necessity of survival and by a primary attribute of mankind: the quality to transmit learning to others. Thus, human behavior becomes normalized within any surviving group. Limits upon permissible behavior tend to stereotype it in many areas other than those directly involved with survival. As music occurs in human groups, so does it exist as culture and is similarly limited. Much of the material in this book will necessarily concern the limits that culture places upon the creative art we call music.

What sort of human activity is music, then? Music can be thought of as a series of characteristics, but some may be absent in certain types of music. Music can be described as a combination of pitch, duration, timbre, melody, patterning and improvisation. However, the pitchless Maori *haka* is still music -- at least to the Maori. The rhythmless funeral dirges of Tikopia are still music. Improvisation is hardly allowed in Western fine art music. What all musics share is the concept of patterned sound, even though the components of the pattern differ from one situation to another.

Music, then, has both biological and cultural limitations, but cannot be defined too tightly. Perception is limited by biological mechanisms and altered by culturally acceptable regularization of sound. As a culturally defined mechanism, music is perceived through cultural canalization and is defined by specific groups who participate in particular genres. It contains silence, interspersed with patterned sound, of which the characteristics vary. It may or may not be a strictly human activity. Such a definition of music is puzzling in that, with the exception of the concept of articulation, this could be defining language. This is deliberate; for the authors believe that music and language represent parts of a continuum of patterned sound, particularly since songs may have texts. The fact is that human beings (and perhaps some other animals) pattern the sounds that disturb the air and others' ears. When this sound is highly regularized, it is frequently called music. Perhaps one day music may be defined more correctly through the tedious process of deciding what music is not.

THE NATURE OF ETHNOMUSICOLOGY

The term, ethnomusicology, has been ascribed to Jaap Kunst, who proposed it in his book of the same name (1955). Earlier scholars whose interests lay in the strictly musicological areas grouped themselves together loosely under the term, *Vergleichende Musikwissenschaft*, "Comparative Musicology". There seems to be no school of thinking connected with the term; the subject of study at first consisted of the "exotic".

Almost all definitions of such earlier studies indicated an interest in the "other" kind of music. Most early definitions involved geographic concepts (Gilman, 1909; Bingham, 1914; Sachs, 1959; Kunst, 1955; Nettl, 1956; Rhodes, 1956; Schneider, 1957), and were rather selective. Bingham suggested that exotic music should include primitive, oriental, and the music of Dalmation peasants (1914). The assumption of all of these definitions is that ethnomusicology confines itself to the study of musics other than that of the fine art system which developed in Western Europe and spread throughout the industrial world.

While such an approach is certainly reasonable (in view of the present situation of musicology, where many scholars labor on the specific problems created by the written art music of Western cultures), the geographical approach to ethnomusicology is still an anomalous one. It implies that there is an "in" and "out", and that never the twain shall meet.

Some scholars have taken a different approach. Alan Merriam (1960, 1964) shows his anthropological bias by the definition of ethnomusicology as "the study of music in culture". Gilbert Chase views ethnomusicology from a more general principle:

> The present emphasis...is on the musical study of contemporary man, to whatever society he may belong, whether primitive or complex, Eastern or Western (1958:7).

Chase goes on to state that "musicology" is now almost entirely a historical discipline, frequently calling itself "historical musicology". The tendency of musicologists in the past few decades has been to restrict their work to composers, artists and performance-oriented impresarios who are no longer living. Chase distinguishes between ethnomusicology as a study of present-day phenomena and musicology as the study of the past. In this perspective, there is no necessary

13

restriction on the geographics of ethnomusicology. This may have influenced Kolinski's assertion that ethnomusicology represents a difference in general approach from musicology (1957).

That these distinctions between musicology and ethnomusicology are more a matter of practice than of theory is well presented by Mantle Hood, who added "ethno-" to the American Musicological Society definition of musicology:

> (Ethno)musicology is a field of knowledge, having as its object the investigation of the art of music as a physical, psychological, aesthetic, and cultural phenomenon. The (ethno)musicologist is a research scholar, and he aims primarily at knowledge about music (1957:2).

From this point of view, ethnomusicology is the study of music, wherever it may be found and can be historical as well. In addition, the concept of music in culture is embodied in the definition.

The authors' definition: ethnomusicology is the study of the music either past or present, of all who participate in music as creators, performers, or hearers of sound patterns; taking into account all factors which lead to a better understanding of this particular type of creative, human display.

MODERN CULTURAL TRENDS

The nineteenth century represents a vital era because

14

new approaches to learning and thinking developed almost simultaneously throughout the Christian world. The most prominent trend -- the full development of the Industrial Revolution -- led eventually to a firm position for the middle-class in the economics of most industrialized countries. At the same time, the nineteenth century saw the final break of the dogmatic hold which had been squeezing scholarship to death for some four hundred years. The Catholic hold on art, morality, ethics and the humanities crumbled under the assault of Charles Darwin as did other Christian doctrines. The restricted content and context for music had already been breaking down; the Protestant movement began the process of secularizing musical forms; new trends in rhythm and harmony were allowed into some liturgies, and even the so-called "Devil's Interval" or tritone (e.g., F-B) began to appear in liturgical music.

The nineteenth century also saw an increase in transportation and communication around the world. Coming on the heels of an established colonialism, adventurers and missionaries grew in number as general wealth increased. This trend brought about a proliferation of material, however badly stated, about the music of people of many cultures.

It is to certain developments in linguistics, however, that ethnomusicology owes the major impetus toward the study of the music of other cultures. The discovery of Sanskrit and its relationship to modern European languages in the nineteenth century gave respectability to the study of non-European cultures as did no other discovery. With the unravelling of Sanskrit came the realization that India was a fully developed civilization as early as the fourteenth century, B. C., a time when even Greece was thought to be barbaric.

15

The linguistic unfolding of the world to study, in this dramatic way, cried for imitation in other human areas. If languages were related, were the arts, or music, poetry, or myth? The stage was set for social Darwinism in all areas pertaining to humanity.

Later in the nineteenth century, linguistics as a study of formal integrity developed fully in the works of Ferdinand de Saussure, whose scholarship (1908, 1916) revolutionized ideas about all levels of language study. Linguistics also led to one of ethnomusicology's most significant tools when the phonetician, A. J. Ellis, developed the Cent system for measuring pitch.

By the end of the nineteenth century, the outreach of the Western world was growing with one startling discovery after another. In archaeology, Ur of the Chaldees, the pyramids of Gizeh, Schliemann's discoveries of Troy and Mycenae brought the glory of gods, graves and scholars into a new prominence. Franz Boas, a geographer, became enthralled with the Eskimo; the sailing ships of the world developed to their full potential; and adventurers and seekers after fortune blundered upon one discovery after another.

The combination of the development of the social sciences and the discovery of art forms of great majesty and beauty naturally led to a new awareness of the world of the West. This was developed further in the twentieth century in such forms as a new humanism (symbolized by the League of Nations and the United Nations), the development of great museums and a subsequent interest in all aspects of the arts from all over the world.

As these events and trends came together, Western

Europe stepped into a new role: more aware, less introspective, less monistic than before. This was not a sudden or extravagant move, since Europe's isolation was broken first by the Crusades; later, by the Renaissance; and finally, by the gathering snowball of forces which led to a more expectant view of the world, which is still maintained today.

It is no longer surprising to find fine art composers, graphic and plastic artists of the Western tradition showing an interest in folk and primitive art and music. With the discovery of the African carving and metal-working traditions, the European fine arts were broken away from formalism and naturalism by the startling discoveries of arts which could be appreciated by Western eyes and ears. While this development had taken place previously in the more philosophical areas, its entry into the world of fine arts was the final stamp of approval on "humanity".

Tinges of condescension were still to be heard. Early writers on music maintained that the music of the other people of the world was simple -- a hang-over from the unilinear evolutionary view of anthropology in the nineteenth century -- and epithets of "crude" and "primitive" were regularly applied to the graphic and plastic arts of others. It took the discovery that behavioral diversity is as great in economically simple cultures as in complex ones to explode the idea of an unbroken development of mankind displayed in the present day by "primitive contemporaries".

The concept of "other" is still very real in the study of non-European music. While this is a general manifestation of scholarship in all disciplines in this century, it seems to be reinforced in the study of the fine arts. One reason may be that Western art music has always been considered an isolatable element which does not depend on cultural trends, economic conditions, or history, but rather on the singular abilities of composers and artists.

Music is psychologically removed from personal lives and considered as a god, but one that is semi-divine. The great composers of the Classical and Romantic periods of Western fine art music are also frequently deemed either divine or semi-divine beings. For example, Charles Seeger quotes a conversation between himself and the eminent musicologist, Manfred Bukofzer, after hearing a session on jazz at a meeting of the American Musicological Society. On leaving the room, Bukofzer remarked, "Those people think jazz is sacred". Seeger said, "Well, you think Bach is sacred, don't you?", to which Bukofzer replied, "Oh, but he is!"

This tendency to view great creators and performers as semi-divine ("the divine diva") may have led musicology to a certain shyness in dealing with *living* creators and performers, and may be responsible for the modern trend to await someone's death before beginning a study of his or her music. But the subject matter is still "holy", and one may think of the musicologist as a person who is handling "sacred" material and who must carry him/herself like a priest. Thus, art music is used as a removal device by those who have been trained to consider it in this manner. One escapes from daily problems by listening to music; one is enlightened or uplifted by great music; or one is re-invigorated and given strength by the thought that humans can create such beauty.

If these assumptions are correct, the development of ethnomusicology lay partly in this tendency to avoid the living composer in the present-day society. The study of "others" is safe; they are outside one's ken and thus beyond the range of one's psychological devices. Musicologists, on the other hand, may view ethnomusicologists as tradition-breakers; after all, they talk to live people who also happen to be creative artists.

Thus, the concept of an "other out there", combined with one's own internal restrictions on the study of present-day creative art, may have led inevitably to the development of something called "ethnomusicology". Are ethnomusicologists a safety valve for aesthetic studies? And if so, what is their position? Are they to be the breakers of tradition and the makers of new traditions? Having personally felt awe of an aesthetic nature in the presence of a great performer in another culture, one can understand how difficult it must be for people sensitive to the beauty of music to work with living composers. The dedication to the concept of music interferes with its study; one finds one's self undone by beauty, caught unawares by it and whirled away. In a sense, it is safe to study traditions not understood, for one is less likely to be psychologically removed from reality by them.

This may be a venture completely new in the history of mankind: the subtle study of aesthetic traditions not one's own, with the aim of understanding them and, thereby, better understanding one's self. This type of study is not exclusively Western; it is wise to remember that others have also studied aesthetic traditions beyond their own. According to the Chinese classic, the *Fze Chun*, the Emperor Chow Wen Whang maintained a bureau for collecting the texts of folk songs throughout China, in order to determine public opinion of government: "Wen Whang gathers folk songs in order to testify his failure or success" (Wang, 1965:312).

Ahmad Faris reported on European music in the

19

nineteenth century. His visits to Malta, England and France led to observations on music which are no more naive than nineteenth-century Western comments on non-European music (Cachia, 1973).

In reporting on the musics of present-day cultures other than the Western or Western-oriented, ethnomusicologists may take two different approaches. First, they may wish to perform music. In so doing, understanding is affected through the learning process, generally of an instrument demanded by a musical system. Students who do field work following this tradition are likely to learn to play instruments and thereby gain knowledge about the musical system with which they are working. Thus, practical music at the university level is generally followed by practical music in the field.

Another method revolves around the concept that music occurs within a social setting, and that a full understanding of music requires an understanding of the sociocultural setting. While the learning of musical instruments is not eschewed, it is not recommended. Thus, persons trained in this system tend to ignore the learning process (for an instrument or for singing) in favor of the more abstract and theoretical approaches characteristic of anthropology.

In both cases, the system of training is oriented toward the same goal: the understanding of music. While neither concentrates exclusively on any one area, there is a tendency for the theoretical premises to reflect the special emphases of each system of training. Students from these two different schools of thought might find themselves reporting on the same society very differently. Neither reflects a complete study of music. In emphasizing the cultural context, much valuable information about the nature of music and the nuances of performances are lost. In emphasizing the learning process, many of the reasons for the performance of music remain unclear.

Not all scholars accept this as a schism. Information about music can come from any reasonable source and should be as wide in scope as possible. In many instances, an ethnomusicologist will be forced into the role of a performer whether this is useful or not. In others, an ethnomusicologist may never learn to perform even upon one instrument within a culture because of the complexity of the musical system being studied. A perfect study has probably never been done, nor has a perfect research design been constructed. What is required by each individual situation often determines the results; what is called for in a scholar is flexibility and diversity.

PRESENT SUCCESSES

One of the most significant aspects of ethnomusicology is the cross-cultural understanding of the nature of music. The realization that music is *not* a universal language, but that it differs markedly from one society to another is a first step. The secondary understanding, that the meaning of music differs radically from one society to another, is not far behind. The statement that yet another human value is provincial, local and culture-bound is not the most pleasant discovery.

The vast accumulation of evidence shows mankind as an exceedingly flexible creature who brings order into life in an infinite variety of ways within the framework of human survival. It is sad, perhaps, to discover that music is not an easy means for bridging cultural chasms; however, in view of the experience of other scientists who have also reached out to the rest of the world, it is not unexpected. Music has no charms to soothe the savage breast, nor yet to instill in all mankind the same values, as Merriam has pointed out (1964).

A slow realization has developed that there must be a constant revision and re-ordering of the consideration of the nature of music. Music represents one of the most puzzling aspects of human behavior. While it changes through time, music retains fragments of information from the past; it also changes at various rates, depending on many factors. While its meanings and values shift from one society to another, the scholar's search for the nature of mankind in this most delicate of areas is enlivened and enriched by the depth of introspection displayed by musicians throughout the world and the dazzling variety of techniques and underlying aesthetic values displayed by its perpetrators. No scholar could ask for more. Music represents one of the most enigmatic, varied and unknown qualities of human life.

Ethhnomusicologists have made the usual mistakes, having tried to patronize music and the musicians of other cultures; having called some primitive, some boring, or limited. There has been a tendency to attempt to force the music of other people into a chronological mold. It is difficult to explain something which is different; without the benefit of terminology, one is lost. However, it is not possible to use a single terminology set for historical musicology of Europe.

As new concepts emerge in other areas of scholarship, there is an attempt to apply them to music. In the near future, undoubtedly, a host of post-Freudian or other borrowed analytical devices will develop for understanding the nature of music, as is presently seen in the influences of structuralism and semiotics.

All of these tendencies in ethnomusicology have one factor in common. They indicate that, as yet, this field has developed no dogma of its own and is not yet molded into a discipline so rigid, that persons interested in the study of music may no longer contribute anything new. This is an important period for these reasons. It is during such moments in the life of a discipline that its best thinking can be done. When scholars work on the edge of an unknown, they frequently transcend themselves, producing work and ideas which would be impossible in a later, more stylized period.

This, then, is the halcyon time for ethnomusicology. There is much to be learned in all areas of the world, through no matter what methodological frame.

CONCLUSION

Ethnomusicology as a discipline is an undefined area of study. Its focus is music. Its scholars may have formal training in several different disciplines. There are no limitations on what may or may not be done and the problems thus far encountered still outnumber the scholars in the field.

As in any other field of study, ethnomusicology has its specialists in certain areas of the world whose information is precious because of its depth, and its few generalists whose contributions encompass aspects of the field as a whole. Thus, ethnomusicology is an area of study with a name with which no one is happy, and an aim of which no one is sure. The work is done in the roistering, rollicking atmosphere of goals too high to reach and problems too large to solve.

This is a situation which always arises when mankind first turns attention to something not previously considered. The breadth of possibilities of study are limited only by the imagination and ability of the scholar. The results are as unpredictable as one would expect creative art to be.

2

CONTEXT AND PERFORMANCE

Music, as implied before, is patterned sound limited by biology and culture. In this chapter, the more specific ramifications of the areas of context and performance will be discussed.

CONTEXT

A context is either that which proceeds or follows an item and thus explains it or the totality in which it is found. A context may be any referent point plus any locus. If two trains are moving near one another, one cannot tell which is moving unless there is a third point of reference. In terms of music, a single pitch is not music when heard in isolation, but becomes music through the accumulation of other points of reference.

"Context" may refer either to the actual time sequence in which an item of music is found (such as the ordering of a ceremony), or to the ideal time sequence in a category of events. Alternately, context may be any aspect of patterned relationships within which the pattern of music is considered apt. For music, contexts are of several orders. They may be geographic contexts such as African music, North American music, Baganda music or Sioux music. Contexts are also seasonal: those involving cyclical events, seasons of the year, or seasons within the human life cycle such as birth, marriage, childbirth, or death.

Time-space relationships may be regarded as a type of context, with the right time and place for the performance of certain kinds of music. The Indian raga determines the improvised pieces; the time of day determines the raga. In Western society, radio stations usually do not broadcast sopranos between 7 and 9 o'clock in the morning, although no one is quite sure why. It is traditional to avoid high-pitched sounds too early in the morning while people are driving to work and listening to the radio.

Statements of "who", "where", "when", "what", "why" and "how" symbolize the types of metaphysical, existential and actual environments (or circumstances) in which music occurs. There is no limit to the number of applications of the concept; context may be as broad or as narrow as the individual researcher desires to make it.

The concept of context is particularly helpful in the study of music, since the tendency, historically, is to emphasize only certain aspects of context. Viewed in the larger sense of the interweaving of parts within a whole, out of which a researcher may choose to investigate any sets of integumental relationships, the concept of context proves exceedingly valuable. Past tendency was to define parts of a culture's music in such terms as drunk songs, gambling songs, war songs, funeral songs, et cetera. This approach, while somewhat useful, breaks down immediately if one begins to study the ways in which a particular society classifies its own music.

Among the Kutenai of northern Idaho, certain gambling songs appear in ritual contexts with appropriate changes in form. Are they gambling songs, then? Are they ritual songs? In fact, they are neither. They are songs to the *nupika*, who bestow good luck. To call them gambling songs or ritual songs is a cover term which may be useful in certain circumstances, but does not aid in the understanding of what music is.

There is also the tendency to define the music of a culture as what that culture does, which can be a tremendous problem. As McAllester inquired, when a Japanese violinist plays Beethoven, is he playing Japanese music? Music crosses cultural boundaries and in some cases, it is redefined when it does so. In other instances, it is not.

The relationship between two cultures is sufficiently complex that entire books on the process of acculturation have graced publishers' lists for years. The implication that a culture may borrow the music of another culture completely destroys the statement that Cherokee music is what the Cherokee *do*. This emphasizes the need for a variety of viewpoints which will destroy old paradoxes. The concept of context helps to unravel such problems, giving a framework of explanation which is extremely useful at all levels of analysis.

One of the most interesting things about music is that it is the most highly patterned form of human behavior. Music is not only highly patterned, but also *staged*. This implies that the pattern called music coincides with certain other aspects of behavior which, themselves, have become patterned as a result.

In some cases, this is called dance; in others, it is called costuming. In yet others, it might be called stagecraft. The fact remains that whenever music occurs, some kinds of behavioral alterations which are patterned and formalized occur with it. Thus, the context of music becomes an indicator of the quality not only of performance, but also of the nature of the human behavior enacted.

The study of context raises a major question: Why do people do this? Like the ritualization of speech in religion or in certain types of expressive culture, music tends to formalize the behavior around it. The study of that formality is one of the most pertinent ways of understanding the music, itself. The authors have called this formalization of behavior "staging" in order to emphasize what is perhaps one of the most fascinating aspects of the study of music.

LEVELS OF CONTEXT

Merriam (1964) mentions that culture is a context. While this is certainly true and it may be wise to begin with the largest level of generalization, the concept of culture is far too diffuse to be of use in every situation. The authors' researches in Malta led to a guitarist nicknamed Il-Bozen, regarded as the natural heir to the great guitarist, Cardona, who was a solo guitarist in the older improvisational style. When singers perform any of the various Maltese musical styles, guitarists interpose an improvised sequence (usually of four phrases in length) between each verse of singing. Il-Bozen, while a traditional guitarist, occasionally uses European melodies as the basis for his improvisations.

At the level of culture as context, then, Il-Bozen could be regarded as an atypical musician. Closer attention to the immediate context of situation in which Il-Bozen used foreign melodies in his improvisations gives another picture. If the singer mentions foreigners in the verse immediately preceding his improvisation, Il-Bozen uses a foreign melody as the basis of his improvisation. In no other context does he do this. One "meaning" of the use of foreign melodies implies that each of Il-Bozen's improvisations may be a coded comment on the verse sung just previously. In this light, Il-Bozen no longer need be considered an atypical musician, but simply an individual musician whose interpretation of a coded system needed to be deciphered.

As can be seen from the above, the immediate context in which a piece of music is performed may be highly significant in explaining what is happening in the music. Not only this, but it is to be expected that there will be levels of contexts for music, both within and without the form, itself. These are powerful explanatory devices for different levels of significance.

At the level of context of culture, the most daring and vocal researcher to date is Alan Lomax (1968). Lomax maintains that there may be an intimate relationship between musical and primarily cultural features, so that a particular orchestration, musical form, voice type, or type of range will be found only in those cultures which exhibit certain cultural features.

For instance, sung music may be performed in different ways with respect to control of the throat and facial muscles.

Sound performance may be augmented by stiffening the muscles of the throat and jaw. Singing "on the diaphragm" produces a variety of sounds, depending upon the opening or closing of various resonators within the head. Singing "on the throat" produces a harsh, constricted tone, characteristic of parts of Italy, Malta, North Africa, Spain and several other parts of the world. Lomax maintains that there is a relationship between singing with the muscles of the throat tightened and the sexual restrictions on women in various cultures. Thus, a musical phenomenon is explained by a cultural one.

It is patent that there is some relation between the culture and the conceiving of music. It is obvious that there will be some relationship which can be postulated and proved by cross-cultural comparison between some aspects of music and some aspects of the culture in which that music is found.

Because of the diversity of culture, it is probably impossible to define the total range of contexts available in the entire world. Context, as has been mentioned before, can be thought of as all those elements which go together to make up a whole. Music has a series of contexts at various levels, each of which may cause shifts within the formal structure of the music, itself. Context, then, is a variety of limiting device.

By beginning with the concept of music and moving outward to the concept of context, undoubtedly it will be found that a particular music responds to more than the one context. Features within the form itself will be found to be responsive to very different contextual or limiting levels.

For example, a given style may be based at least partly upon the historical context of the sounds already chosen as music. In addition, the instruments which are used will be those which are available and allowable. The persons who play the style will depend upon the nature of the status of musicians and cultural limitations -- such as who may or may not become a musician. Thus, there will be a series of tangential influences upon music, some on intersecting planes. The idea is to conceptualize an unknown in each case which is knowable, complex and flexible. To do this, one must have a starting point or points which will lead to an increasing perception of the whole.

PHYSICAL CONTEXTS

One of the most fascinating things about the study of music is the way in which performers stretch the concept of the physical limitations of the human body in the performance of music. Ordinarily, it is assumed that women cannot sing bass, nor can men sing soprano unless castrated. Yet in every society, there are voice types which require some members of the community to actually expand their physical limitations in order to achieve the style.

If a tenor voice for women is favored in a given society, as it certainly is in many parts of Eastern Europe, then a selective process will take place unless women's voices can be lowered. In portions of North Africa and in Malta, men preferably should sing in the soprano range, without resorting to falsetto. Some singers can achieve this; others cannot.

There are clearly some physical limitations on what can be done with the human hand, the human voice, and the embouchure of the human mouth. Depending upon the complexity and rigidity of a particular style, some degree of physical mutation will be necessary. String players must develop calluses on their fingers. Every violinist who works at his/her craft will have a scar on the left shoulder. Some musicians must grow long fingernails, while others must keep them short. To the practiced eye, there are often physical signs which accompany the context of instrument player.

This is a wide field of investigation which has hardly been touched by scholars. The extensions and accommodations which music requires of the human frame can potentially serve as potent indicators of limitations of music within the physical realm. In addition, knowledge of the bodily alterations caused by particular instruments can be a valuable aid to a scholar trying to locate musicians in the field.

SOCIAL CONTEXTS

In the broadest sense, separating the cultural from the social context is impossible. For the time being, the assumption will be used that all contexts which are social in nature have to do with the structure of social relations between individuals within a culture. These limitations seem to relate primarily to the question: Who may become a musician?

In Madagascar, there is great variance in the status of musicians. On the high plateau, the Merina and the Betsileo have developed singers who are highly regarded. For the Merina, this results in an upward movement of musicians in the stratified society; while among the Betsileo, musicians arise out of the class of classless men who do not fit into the social status at all (c.f. McLeod, 1964). In the southern desert, musicians are identifiable by living beyond the garbage dumps of any settlement. They are of the lowest class and can display behavior which is unacceptable to all other members of the society.

Where musicians arise from lower classes or from the classless strata in society, not all members of the culture may wish to participate in musical activity because of the pressures which will be placed upon them socially. Obviously, this restricts the number of people who will enter into the musical craft, reducing innovation because fewer people will engage in the trade. Similar pressures undoubtedly exist when a musical style is regarded as the province of upper class individuals.

In Malta, folk music is mainly the province of the lower class. This has not restricted certain members of the upper class from engaging in it, but family pressure is placed upon men who desire to sing to cease and desist. One sad example was that of a contractor who sang briefly in his youth, until his wife objected violently. After her death, he attempted to re-enter the musical community where he was welcomed. Unfortunately by this time, he was an old man and could no longer take the pressures of constant improvisation and soon dropped out.

Where a style is difficult, as in the Maltese, the end result may be that fine minds, like the gentleman above, may not be able to add their genius to the repertoire through purely social factors. It is important to recognize the nature of social factors. In particular, those constraints which limit or define the population of musicians should be noted, as should any sanctions on the nature of music or its audiences.

LINGUISTIC CONTEXT

As Durbin has pointed out (1971), music and linguistic texts which accompany music interweave with one another in a special way. Shifts in grammar of major proportions occur regularly between conversational speech and poetic speech. Poetic speech is the very basis of musical texts; but even between poetic speech and song, certain shifts may be expected. Sometimes, burden syllables or other devices for allowing musical rhythms to take precedence over poetic meter are used. Thus, language changes in the context of music. In the same sense, music changes in the context of text.

In the song, "Zadoahy", quoted by McLeod (1966) and Herndon (1974), long duration, high tone and heavy accent occur in conjunction with diphthongs or silent consonants. Thus, music is constrained by text as well as the other way around. This relationship -- such an acute one for the study of music -- deserves serious consideration. One of the most significant factors for the formation of style may lie in text rather than in tune. While this is not a one-to-one relationship, it is clear that in some cases, music takes precedence over text, while the reverse is true in others. The unscrambling of this particular problem is perhaps one of the most interesting challenges available to ethnomusicologists.

THE OCCASION AS CONTEXT

Of all the explanatory devices used by the authors, the concept of the occasion has proved to be the most powerful. While songs can be studied in any manner, one of the most revealing ways is through the occasions upon which music occurs. This is not a theoretical concept; rather, it is a methodological one.

The occasion may be defined as the point of focus encompassing the perception, performance, or creation of music. The occasion includes what Westerners call performances, but is not restricted to formal events.

It is assumed that there will be something similar about all occasions of a particular type upon which music occurs; one of the similarities may be the kind of music which is performed. While this idea is simple, it has extensive ramifications as far as the concepts of repertoire, ceremony, ritual ordering and specialized personnel are concerned.

The question, then, is "*When* is music?" In dealing with the occasion as context, both the so-called "native" categories and the scholar's viewpoint are involved. That is, not only those events in a culture's expression which are named or otherwise marked by it as points in time on which it is to be expected, but also those events which may be recognized by the scholar as having musical interest, whether the group concerned recognizes them as such or not.

As a behavioral phenomenon, the occasion includes the full range of human performances and includes not only such informal events as a picnic, but also formalized events such as concerts or coronations. It is to be expected that in some instances, it will be the informal events which provide insight into the more formal occasions, since the latter are often complex and difficult to follow.

One of the best examples of the way in which the concept of the occasion may be useful is to be found in the Hungarian Harvest Festival in Louisiana. This event occurs at the end of the harvest season as a way of offering a thanksgiving. A hall is decorated with fruit, flowers and vegetables; children come dressed in their native costumes. A band is assembled, usually consisting of a violin or two, clarinet and *czimbalom* (the struck zither) and such other instruments as may be available. The members of the community come for two reasons: to see one another and to watch the dancing of old Hungarian dances by the young people dressed in their special costumes. Chief among these dances is the *Czardas*.

Although many points of reference can be mentioned here, only one will be pointed out. Song texts, especially the *Czardas*, tend to emphasize beautiful young girls. Traditionally, for a Hungarian, the most desirable female in the world is between twelve and fourteen years old. Women are considered to have lost their beauty once the peach fuzz disappears from their cheeks.

In the Harvest Festival, the problems of Hungarian marriages are portrayed. Here, the beauty of youth is extolled in song, but the beautiful young girls are rebuffed by those whom they would like to meet, for men must avoid women of marriageable age. Bachelors are not masters of their own fates and the songs portray this in many ways.

The poignancy of songs, the talk of ripening wheat, of brightness and gaiety is combined with talk of great sadness. Traditionally, fathers and brothers must avoid their daughters and sisters in public; potential husbands must do so as well, for no one is in control of this situation. Here can be seen one of the most important principles of the occasion: that of the presence within music of ideas which are too socially dangerous to handle. The extreme segregation to be found in the Hungarian Harvest Festival is probably the result of

36

strain within the family as well as the rivalry among the matriarchs for pride of place. Seating is done strictly according to status within the community, especially among matriarchs.

Given the importance of sexuality, it is publicly stated in song and because of the fact that no one controls it well, it is stated musically rather than verbally. The occasion for this music in this community, the Harvest Festival, brings out all aspects of the nature of womanly beauty and displays them in more or less rigid form for the community, itself.

The range of information which may be discerned from a concentration upon the musical occasion as the context for musical activity is wide and unpredictable. The scholar may be dealing with very small or extremely large numbers of people in attempting to study a single event. It cannot be predicted with any degree of certainty what kind of information will be gleaned from a particular study, but the nature of one's understanding about a particular music will undoubtedly be deepened through continued focus on musical events and occasions.

THE INDIVIDUAL AS CONTEXT

It has previously been mentioned that there is a distinction to be made between performing music and simply hearing it. An individual may, at different times, have different degrees of involvement in music. This, like the occasion, is a simplistic statement; however, it is an extremely important one.

The individual scholar can, through continued observation of a number of contexts and on many occasions, provide him/herself an area for better comprehension of the range of aesthetic experiences in a given culture. As anyone who has ever listened to music knows, one's reaction to music differs depending on where one is and how one feels. A person's reaction to music also depends on *who* that person is.

An individual is a context in any sense in which the individual finds him/herself. If the person is purely a listener, then it is through his/her mind that the music must be appreciated and judged. Each culture teaches its members how best to judge music and the other arts, in more or less well organized verbal statements.

Western society tends to isolate performers from audiences in many ways, calling its opera singers "divine" and staying away from them. This is currently changing; but in the 1930's and 1940's, it was common practice for great singers to be given favored tables in restaurants; to be protected by special cars, drivers, clothing, and escorts; to be lauded with flowers; to be surrounded by helpers of various kinds. Today's working opera star does not have to endure this as much; however, even today the cult of awe does surround these ladies and gentlemen to some extent. She is called "diva" or "divine diva"; he is called "master" or "maestro". In other societies, a listener may have a more casual approach to performers.

Just as music may be isolated, the performers of music may be isolated. As a result, the audience is segregated from the performer in some situations, but in some societies this may not be the case. In Malta, a fine performer may be the object of direct contact with his listeners in many ways. As one singer said, "If I hear a fine man sing, I want to go up and shake his hand". When this gentleman was given an explanation of the way in which American performers are sometimes treated, he said thoughtfully, "So that's why they assassinated President Kennedy". He felt the same appreciation of a fine performer as anyone might, but his reaction was completely different.

The varieties of involvement of an individual in performance may differ radically from those found in Western society, with its segregation of performer and audience. In Malta the word, *dilettant*, is used to describe both those who sing and those who love to listen to music. It is easy to slide from one "status" to another; the ranks of performers are drawn more easily from the ranks of listeners. There are many occasions when individuals from the audience are asked if they wish to sing; young children are tolerated in singing situations or occasions. Singers are noted for their permissiveness; even women may sometimes join in singing if they so desire.

The point of view of the actual performer is again different from that of the individual who stands outside. The performer is in better command of the rules and regulations by which he or she performs and has a better grasp of where he or she stands within the musical milieu. In another respect, the performer has a narrower point of view; he or she is often compelled by an inner desire to perform.

Each individual has as his or her context for music a different point of view. Those who would study this phenomenon can learn much from speaking with introspective people who are listeners, as well as those who are performers of good music.

Some people are taken unaware by musical forms they

have never heard before. McLeod (in Herndon and Brunyate, 1976) reports a case in point of a woman at an opera film. She had come to the movies early in the afternoon and was unable to leave the theater. She had to keep returning to the theater to hear the beautiful music, but was then so compelled to cry that she rushed into the ladies' room and burst into sobs, and had been so reacting for five hours. She had never heard an opera before and had come upon the great beauty of Italian opera suddenly without preparation. The woman was a member of the lower class and had not been taught that it was acceptable behavior to cry in a theater.

Music is a powerful tug on human emotions. It would be foolish to ignore the fact that almost all listeners and almost all performers are compelled to do what they do by inner feelings too strong to ignore. This is dealing with emotions; when these are the subject of study, it is to the kinesic that one must turn for information.

KINESICS

Mention has been made above of the Hungarian community and the division of the community by status and sex within the hall; these are examples of "kinesics", the way in which people move in order to demonstrate their position within a community. In the same way that other people display their roles and status by the way in which they move and hold their bodies, musicians also have revealing kinesic indicators.

McLeod mentions for Madagascar (1964) that musicians are allowed more extensive behavior than other members of the community because of their association with ritual danger. It is uncommon to see a Malagasy normally using completely open arm gestures; musicians, however, do so. Bear hugs are even common among Malagasy musicians.

In every community, some kind of special behavior marks the musician as such. White jazz musicians frequently are "night people" and have little or nothing to do with normal society, demonstrated both verbally and in kinesics. Jazz musicians frequently form barriers between themselves and the audience; they often wear sunglasses and refuse to look directly at their patrons. The back of the piano is often placed toward the audience and the musicians huddle behind it; huge music stands are placed on the stage. All these gestures and manipulations of space indicate aversion, a fact which can be verified by the speech patterns of musicians, who use in-group dialects and who refer to their listeners with contempt and condescension.

Musicians throughout the world have their own ways of expressing themselves. Much of what they say with their bodies is a direct result of the kind of music they perform. Jazz, for instance, was regarded as evil in the early part of the century (c.f. Merriam, 1964). This caused people interested in performing jazz to take on the characteristics they believed to be associated with it -- i.e., difference from the ordinary.

Musicians know that the performing of music is a passion. Most of them also know that the public display of passion must be handled carefully and kept firmly under control. The way in which musicians move in order to do this is frequently an indication of the basic values which the music represents for the community. If nothing whatsoever was known about Western classical music, it could be guessed that it is a historical phenomenon from the fact that musicians on the stage wear clothing styles which went out of fashion

41

twenty to fifty years ago, depending upon the community. The tendency to play music by persons who are dead and to revere them greatly is another part of the cycle of values which surrounds Western music.

Musicians, then, act out their parts. The blues singer who looks only at his guitar is clearly indicating that nothing is there but his guitar. The jazz musician who hides behind a music stand is saying that he is going to play another way, in spite of what people think about his music. The violinist who glorifies dead composers does so in clothing and with gestures from the past.

In some cases, musicians act their parts so well that the whole central meaning of a musical system may be acted out before the eyes of the observer. In Malta, one of the more heavily populated areas of the world, it is normal for people to have very small space envelopes around them. The Maltese live close to one another by choice as well as necessity. Crowds are intense; but musicians demand and receive an exceptionally wide space around them. Two musicians who are singing to each other may be found at either end of a long room, or with the barrier of a table between them. People back away from their bodies; singers never look at one another. They look at the ceiling or play with matches or gloves, look down at their hands, or generally avoid eye contact.

What are they saying with these gestures? If one looks at the music, one finds that the variety of music being sung is the song duel of Malta in which two men attempt to cleverly insult one another in public. The fact that these are insult songs helps to explain the very wide space envelope and the aversion gestures so common to individuals singing this

42

variety of music (for an example of this form in English, see Herndon and Brunyate, 1976).

The kinesics of musicians are frequently helpful in understanding the nature of the music created and sung, particularly if their body movements and gestures are compared with those of the general public. So fascinating is this study with so little done about it, that the authors wish to stress it as a field of study well worth investigating.

PERFORMANCE

The concept of the occasion mentioned above involves the performance of music in a context. This is an obvious concept, but one which moves away from simply emphasizing music *per se*. This concept differs slightly from that of music as "song in culture", in that there is a focus upon the moment of performance. But what is performance? How may the concept of performance be integrated in ways that are useful? How might it be distinguished from the concept of the occasion?

The first mention of this usage is that of Milton Singer when he speaks of the "cultural performance":

> ..."cultural performances" include
> what we in the West usually call
> by that name -- for example, plays,
> music concerts and lectures. But
> they also include prayers, ritual
> readings and recitations, rites and
> ceremonies, festivals and all those
> things which we usually classify
> under religion and ritual rather

43

than with the "cultural" or artistic (1955:23).

For Singer, a cultural performance has a specified time limit with a beginning and an end, an organized program of activity, a set of performers, an audience, a place, and a pre-specified occasion for performance. Still focusing on the context in which music is performed (by using Singer's approach), those occasions would be included which are fairly tightly organized. Many occasions for the performance of music, such as singing a child to sleep with a lullaby, game playing, singing to one's self, cannot be included in this approach. Singer chooses the more tightly organized aspects of musical occasion to be singled out because these are generally isolatable segments of activity. He asserts that they demonstrate cultural encapsulation of basic ideas.

This accords well with the very definition of the term "performance". When a cultural performance takes place, elements of culture are presented to the carriers of that culture in highly symbolized forms, supposedly to demonstrate basic ideals and principles upon which society operates. As Herndon stated, "...he views cultural performances as isolatable segments of activity considered by a group of people to be encapsulations of their culture which they exhibit to visitors and themselves (1971:339).

Singer's view is important in that it implies that highly formalized human behavior is a cultural focus and that it is probably symbolic and meaningful on several levels. It is commonplace that public presentations are usually symbolic re-statements of some kind. The repetitiveness of art forms implies that something is being told, whether words are involved or not. By including the concepts of ritual, rites and

44

ceremonies, Singer extends the concept of performance into a social statement about mankind which is probably valid. The distinction between play and ritual is slight; both have role-playing, costuming, an order of performance, proper words which must be said in the proper sequence, et cetera. Play and ritual, both, involve standardized speech, behavior and, frequently, standardized settings.

This view looks at the occasion for music from the structural point of view, as does the concept of occasion. Abrahams (1976) has discussed performance in terms of social interactions, which is a difficult task. He has distinguished between performance and normal behavior on grounds similar to Singer's, but focuses on quality rather than on time or setting.

The concept of social interaction implies that for a performance to occur, there must be more than one person involved, either in terms of two or more performers, or one performer with an audience. According to this conceptualization, performances may occur only on approved and accepted occasions; only certain members of the community will have license to perform; a framing device will be present to indicate that this is a different type of behavior; a repertoire of actual performance items must be slotted in which the requirement of the generic expectations involved will be fulfilled. Thus, for a performance to occur, there must be a coming-together of acknowledged performers, marked times, places, occasions and a repertoire. This is what Abrahams calls "pure" performance.

Like Singer, Abrahams' definition implies that for an activity to be a performance, there are strict patterns of expectations: more than one person, and a high level of stereotypic behavior on the part of performers and listeners alike. The stress is laid upon the "something special" about times and places when performances occur and the heavy formalization involved. Singer focuses on the facts of culture; Abrahams on the behavior of interacting individuals. Each of these concepts is complementary to the other, and each has its place in the study of music.

Richard Bauman holds a similar view, stressing the more formalized aspects of behavior: "...the act of performance as situated behavior, situated within and rendered meaningful with reference to relevant contexts. Context is another way that performance is patterned in communities". Contexts, says Bauman, may be identified as a variety of levels. Religion, education and politics may be viewed from the perspective in which they do or do not represent contexts for performance within communities (1976:35).

Bauman goes on to clarify the concept of performance through a behavior term, "event" -- "a culturally-defined, bounded segment of the flow of behavior and experience that constitutes a meaningful context for action" (loc. cit.). He assumes that Singer's cultural performances are obligatory performances, whether organized for entertainment or some other purpose. He mentions other situations in which events are non-obligatory or optional, but not unexpected, as the telling of jokes at a party. He also discusses ranges of events where performance is not a relevant variable -- not fully categorized within a culture.

This latter view is very helpful in that it distinguishes between types of performance. The authors would tend to accept this concept as similar to the concept of occasion in that whenever something musical happens, the investigator will observe it.

In the definitions of both Singer and Abrahams, the concept is too tight to include all the times and places when music can occur. More importantly, Abrahams' definition omits all occasions in which there is only a single individual performing music. It would be impossible within his definition to discuss the famous American Indian example, the Vision Quest of the Plains Indians. Here, young boys isolate themselves for a number of days -- fasting and praying -- in order to receive power from the Guardian Spirits in the form of songs.

Abrahams would question whether the Vision Quest is a musical performance since no human audience is present, and no social interaction takes place. Singer might include the Vision Quest in the concept of cultural performance, even though the time and place are not well organized and the order of events may not be very clear. Bauman would undoubtedly include this as a performance of music. It would certainly be an occasion for music under the somewhat simplistic definition the authors present here.

For the authors, performance should not be tightly defined: it should include full consideration of all those moments in time in which music occurs. This is a necessary preliminary step to the understanding of the context of music. If one does not discuss all the contexts in which music occurs, one can hardly do a reasonable study of music in context.

How can performance be helpful in the study of ethnomusicology? Probably the major usefulness of this concept is to point out that music is highly patterned and is frequently found in contexts which are highly patterned. Thus, the concept of performance may be one of the focuses of the field. Since this emphasis is synchronic, the concept of performance is both a theoretical and descriptive device -- not of the broadest possible application -- but still useful. It stands in contrast to the concept of performance practice which implies only the study of music.

The study of performance includes both performance practice and its contexts. Performance is the most obvious of the synchronic, syntagmatic views of context. While students of the fine arts may content themselves with the study of manuscripts, ethnomusicologists must study performance of music, since that may be all there is in a community.

If one wishes to study the way in which music is used in a given society, the first test under this approach would be to determine the names of various types of occasions. Every society has not only names and genres for styles, but also named occasions for the performance of music.

Every musician can describe a normalized version of the setting in which music takes place, including the kinds of people who attend to listen, the kinds of people who will sing in different settings, the kinds of settings themselves, the limitations on those settings, et cetera. The presence of named occasions indicates that at least some degree of cultural formalization has already taken place. Once this is known, one may ask to be taken to a named occasion and to observe that particular idiosyncratic set of events.

Subsequent study of similar examples of named occasions will produce a normalized statement which can be checked against specific occasions. One may consider the rigidity of repertoire, of personnel, of audience and of general behavior in a setting which is already formalized. This is the easiest way to approach the kind of music which only disturbs the air and other people's ears, but which has never been set down on paper.

Once these more highly formalized contexts have been understood, one may then move to the study of the less formal occasions on which music occurs. These will be more difficult to acquire since they usually occur intermittently and frequently in private. With some kind of approach already instilled into the music of a given culture, it is not difficult to find and to record those occasions on which music is less formal.

The authors' own experience in the study of these less formal occasions is that it is frequently necessary to make recordings of the music out of context. For instance, while they have some contextual recordings of children's songs, most of these songs were recorded out of context. The same is true of nursery rhymes and lullabies.

The significance of the distinction between the highly organized and the less well organized, the public and the private performance, can be discovered in any society provided that a framework includes all the types available. This is the only reasonable view of an entire community of music. In the less formalized occasions for the performance of music will be included rehearsals, lessons or training sessions and practice. Each of these moments when music is performed has its own validity in which music is created, presented or conceptualized.

In the authors' view, the concept of occasion and its sub-set, that of performance, is a powerful organizing principle by which the vast majority of information about the nature of music, as such, can be gathered. It is a methodological frame into which music may be placed or from which music can be withdrawn for analysis. The interplay between the situation in which music occurs and the musical event itself or, in Abrahams' terms, between performance and performance items, is the study of form in performance.

As mentioned above in the case of Il-Bozen, the context (in this case, musical and textual) in which guitar improvisations take place in the song duel, dictates some of the melodic content of the improvisation. While this is on another level from the concept of performance, it is apparent how this approach illustrates the concept of "contexts within contexts".

CONCLUSION

This chapter has attempted to discuss music as a focus of study and context as a referent and locus of music. The concept of context has been emphasized as an interweaving of factors, one of which is music. The concept of context has led to an understanding of limitations as a way of viewing musical performances. Certain limitations have been mentioned, such as the physical, social, linguistic and cultural. The more specific situational limitations, such as the occasion and performance, have been discussed. All of these approaches move away from the simple emphasis on music, *per se*, which, it is felt, has only minimal usefulness in the study of music.

It was popular some years ago to assume that the only

meaning which music has lies in its form. This emphasis, clearly a result of the view of music as an isolated element, has proven to be less valid than was hoped. The contextual view may also prove to have its limitations; currently, however, the ideas presented here seem to have the most explanatory power of any which the authors have investigated.

All the ethnomusicologist has to work with is the moment in which a piece of music is performed. This is so because there usually is no score from which to work or no manuscript. All that exists for an ethnomusicologist is the performance. The more one knows about performance, the better one will understand music.

3

THE LEARNING PROCESS, MYTH, AND KINESICS

This chapter deals with those aspects of culture which shape and surround music. As a cultural expression and arbitrary patterning of sound, music must be learned by a human group. Learning occurs at many levels, taking a variety of forms. In the process of learning, performing and hearing music, much surrounding myth is created. Additionally, the playing of music, as mentioned earlier, requires movement which is frequently a sort of dance. This chapter will be concerned with some of the mental processes and aspects of context which relate to the learning process, myth, and kinesics.

THE LEARNING PROCESS

The learning process is not a simple matter for it involves not only how performers and creators learn their respective crafts, but also how hearers learn. It is not restricted to the training of the young, but is an ongoing process which continues throughout an individual's lifetime. It is possible to consider learning as a process within the context of human awareness.

The learning process may be formal or informal, obligatory or voluntary, aural or non-aural. Whatever may be involved in the learning process in a particularistic sense, all learning at a given point in time is a consequence of the tonal preferences and the history of a particular group who is teaching the music. The learning process involves what anthropologists have called "enculturation". Enculturation, briefly, is a term which means the development, through the influences of members of a society, of patterns of behavior in children or outsiders that conform to the standards deemed appropriate by the culture. Enculturation or "socialization", as it is often called, incorporates all means of learning of behavioral patterns.

Musical enculturation includes all forms of acquisition of increasing awareness of a specific society's musical sound, behavior, music appreciation and comprehension. Within this concept, one may point to more formalized methods of learning, such as schooling, which includes all forms of intentional instruction, and education, which includes instruction given by individuals recognized as specialists -- removed usually some distance from the student's home and located in a specifically named place. While all music learning involves enculturation, only some may involve schooling or education.

In acquiring competence in dealing with music, it is again necessary to distinguish between those who actively participate and those who do not. In both cases, the designations cited above apply. In some societies, musicians learn to play an instrument, dance, sing, or listen to a style of music through formal lessons; in others, the entire process is informal.

In Western society, it is common for an aspiring composer or performer to spend a number of years in formal student/teacher relationships. Western audiences are not always exposed to the formality of music appreciation classes and tend to acquire their tastes informally. Some styles of Western music are performed by persons who have not received formal lessons, but it is probably safe to say that all Western musicians who perform in the so-called high art traditions (such as opera, symphony and ballet) have encountered formal lessons.

The music learning process may be obligatory or voluntary. If the acquisition of musical competence is obligatory, it is much more likely that the requisite aspect of the process will be directed toward the performers or composers than toward audiences. In Tikopia, it is necessary for chiefs to compose songs at certain periods of their life cycles, whether they are musically inclined or not. It is a matter of rank, birth and status which dictates the obligatory assumption of musical competence to the point of being able to compose a song. It should be pointed out that if the chief is an inadequate composer, he will hire a "ghost writer" to perform the task for him.

Another type of obligatory learning process is involved with aspects of status alone, and may be best illustrated by the common practice of certain American middle class families who felt their children should be forced to learn to play the piano, despite protest from the children (and sometimes from their instructors). Some children learn to play a particular instrument, to dance, or to sing as a voluntary act rather than an obligatory one.

There are probably as many ways to learn a musical style, instrument, or genre as there are people to learn them. It has been demonstrated by Suzuki and Alvin for the violin and the 'cello, respectively, that the enculturation of young children in music behavior is best done aurally. Both methods train children of four or five years of age to play stringed instruments through a combination of carefully designed encouragements to "make a beautiful sound". Through a well-designed series of steps, emphasis is placed on the enjoyable achievement involved in making a tone sound good. Children begin immediately to play Western classical pieces, although difficulties are omitted at first. Students develop a consciousness of tone and pitch as well as an enjoyment of the process of making music. It might be said that, at least for young children, the aural method of instruction produces more rapid results.

Teaching by methods which are not aural, but usually written, can take place either with or without the presence of a teacher. It was long the practice of aspiring Country and Western musicians to send for an instrument and instruction book. In the 1920's and 1930's, the Sears Roebuck catalogue was responsible for the fostering of much interest and learning of music throughout the United States.

It is necessary to distinguish between aural and oral means of learning. With many teachers throughout the world, some degree of verbalization of concepts or desired effects will be made to the student. These verbalizations are, of course, oral. In contrast, aural statements may include performances by a teacher, record, radio broadcasts, films, other media, or live performances. The aural experience may or may not have verbal clues or instruction accompanying it.

It would seem logical that the initial acquisition of musical competence by both hearers and performers should have received more scholarly attention, although this has not been the case. Until recently, little attention was placed upon children's acquisition of verbal or musical skill, and almost no attention was given to the development of children's motor abilities in order to know what areas of physical exertion might be helpful and which might be harmful at a given state of maturity. There has been an increase of scholarly interest in this area; but for music, such studies are relatively new.

In Malta, children learn their musical competence in an informal, voluntary, aural manner. Although there is some encouragement of male children whose fathers or uncles are well-known singers, children are not pressed to become musicians. Infants and young boys, as well as the occasional young girl, often accompany their older male relatives to the bars where singing takes place. The entire family hears traditional Maltese music on many occasions and is generally exposed to the Maltese song duel on an average of one to two hours a week. On their way to school, children often sing verses at one another which are sometimes insulting, and which approach the style of adults to a certain degree.

At other times, a Maltese mother may tell her son to go to the roof of her house to sing an insulting verse or two at an offensive neighbor. Older children are encouraged, if they so desire, to sing with the adult males on certain occasions. If they prove to be good, they are given encouragement and

56

advice regarding singing strategy and may take their places with the men as soon as they are capable. Guitarists, in contrast, often apprentice themselves during adolescence to a master guitarist in a more formal student/teacher relationship.

Children's songs, games and dances have received some attention, particularly in the literature of folklore. These genres have not been treated thoroughly with regard to aspects of the learning process. It is hoped that further work will be undertaken in this area.

HOW AUDIENCES LEARN

A distinction can be made between the learning process necessitated by being a member of the audience, or a hearer of music, and the acquisition of competence in the performance of music. Since the hearing of music is common to both performers and audience, if a layman were asked, "What is an audience?" the response would probably be one of incredulity. Yet, the nature of music as a process taking place through time and aiming at an audience, would seem to indicate that at least as much emphasis should be placed on the audience as is placed on the performer or the composer. An audience is the person or persons who hear the process through time of those aspects of patterned sound which is called music.

There are many types of audience; however, the basic distinction to be made involves the question of whether or not the audience is separate from the performers. Audience responses involve a range of obligatory and possible behaviors, whether the audience is isolated from the performers or not. In urban situations, it is necessary to consider the unique set of problems posed by the distant audience; for when sophisticated recording devices and broadcasting media make possible the hearing or viewing of performances separated in time and place from the actual origin of the sound, the audience is enlarged and diversified. It is an audience, nevertheless, and must be dealt with.

It is also necessary to consider the range of both actual and potential reactions of audiences to various genres of music. Some societies have music designed more as background than as actual sound events to be listened to carefully. A prime example of background music is to be found in Western society in the ubiquitous sound of "Muzak" and other commercial background music systems which inundate America. Background music is also a frequent accompaniment of dining or courtship. The idea of background music is certainly not a new one, nor is it confined to Western society.

Audiences tend to take their cues from particular contexts; their reactions are defined, delimited and constrained by the nature of the occasion. Those who stray from approved audience behavior in any given context soon learn what behavior is appropriate.

This is especially true of more formalized situations. The acute embarrassment of a neophyte concert-goer, applauding vigorously after the first movement of a string quartet and greeted by icy stares from all around the audience, is an intense and immediate learning experience. Anyone with the audacity or the lack of foresight to arrive improperly dressed or to behave incorrectly, will soon receive the negative criticism of other members of the audience and, in some instances, may be forcibly ejected from the premises of a musical event if his or her behavior is too unsuitable. On a simply formalistic level, audience behavior is not usually formally learned, but is the product of the process of enculturation which takes place at the experiential level.

Audience reaction is based, in part, upon the degree of audience sophistication with regard to the particular type of performance which is taking place. With a large audience, it is to be expected that there will be a range of sophistication from untutored, disinterested individuals to a set of devoted admirers. These devotees may or may not possess a formal sophistication regarding the structure of music, or they may be so transported by their own expectations that they are unable to hear the actual sound. These factors must be taken into consideration in any evaluation of audience behavior, reaction, or conceptual relationships within a formal design framework.

HOW PERFORMERS AND CREATORS LEARN

As soon as the question of how performers and creators learn is considered, the concept of talent arises. Very little is known of talent outside of the fine art traditions of Western Europe, India, Southeast Asia, China and Japan. Part of the lack of knowledge about the question of talent has probably arisen from the assumption that in those areas of the world lacking a fine art or high art music, "group performance" is the rule rather than the exception. A perusal of ethnomusicological studies will disprove this assumption at once; music requires certain special capabilities in every society, even the smallest.

The problem of the definition of talent is immense. This can best be brought home by a discussion of the "naturally talented" children in Western society. Many children learn music with an immediacy which is almost uncanny. Taken to church on a Sunday morning, they will listen to the hymns, return home and play them on the piano. For these children, there is an immediate relationship between hearing and reproducing sound. They learn so quickly that they do not have the patience to learn to play well, oftentimes; they simply learn to play.

The immediacy of transfer from hearing to performing is not only the imitation of a particular piece, but also the imitation of styles. Some youngsters can be asked "to play like Beethoven", "play like Wagner", or "play like Sweet Emma the Bell Girl", and they will be able to reproduce a style without necessarily reproducing a piece. The noted concert pianist, Sylvia Zaremba, adds another facet to this information. At about age thirteen, she had to re-learn her entire repertoire because she found she could no longer memorize in the same way as in the past. Her new method of memorization involved visually learning bits of music, rather than simply hearing it and reproducing it.

Two points of reference arise here. First, it may be that there is a dysfunctional relationship between certain types of musical "talent" and normal teaching procedures. Second, there may be a shift in learning method at some point in adolescence; it could be postulated that our society loses many of its talented youngsters through one or another of these experiences. This would imply that each culture chooses from its pool of talented youngsters those who can learn within its precepts and ignores those who cannot.

Western society offers two choices regarding musical expression. The fine art tradition stresses the written musical score and a highly involved teaching method which is progressive in nature. In the popular music field, however, those who have more aural than visual perception listen to recordings hour after hour until they have caught the style they choose to play. They then build upon their knowledge through performance, either alone or in small groups. If this is the case, then the visually-oriented would tend more toward the fine arts, while the aurally-oriented individual would tend more toward popular music.

All of this makes the assumption that there is such a thing as talent. The question of talent, however, must remain moot. Each culture expresses certain qualities which it prefers its musicians to have. Those within the society who live up to those qualities or who possess them may be called "talented". Those who do not, do not become musicians. Cultural ideals are interposed between the individual and the music.

An example from Malta will illustrate this well. In order to become a singer of the style called *spirtu pront*, or song duel, an individual must have the following qualities, according to the singers: cunning, genius, drive, courage and self-discipline. Of these, the most important is genius, for without it, none of the others matter. The genius in question is the ability to improvise verses within the space of 20 seconds, which will follow the complex maze of rules proscribed upon linguistic texts. It is convenient if the man who chooses to sing *spirtu pront* can sing soprano, the primary criterion for a beautiful voice. If he cannot, but yet has the mind to create beautifully shaped verses within the rules and regulations of the style, he is still regarded as a good singer.

61

One of the major criteria for musical talent in Malta is poetic ability of a highly refined and complex sort. In this way, the culture interposes itself between musical "talent" and the final product by shaping the music in the fashion it desires.

HOW PERFORMERS LEARN

There are several methods of learning presently in use throughout the world. The validity of each method depends partly upon the musical style being learned, its complexity and the amount of improvisation involved within it. The most common type is teaching by example. Here, beginning performers learn by listening to a teacher playing at full speed. This is the method of teaching the *valiha* or tube zither of Madagascar. The implication of such a method is that an individual has already learned something about the music and its instrumentation before he or she begins.

Among the Merina, musicians frequently make instruments; young people wishing to learn will often sit with a musician in the marketplace, playing one *valiha* after another. When business grows slack, the teacher will pick up an instrument and play, saying little or nothing; the student imitating whatever has been played. Young men can spend several hours a day at this engaging trade and, after some time, they become quite proficient, branching out on their own and trying new songs. This teaching method is more frequently found with the study of instruments and in areas where set pieces are the norm.

Another variety of learning procedure is that which might be called "teaching by metaphor". Certain movements which are necessary to the creation of the proper sound seemingly cannot be taught directly. Verbalizing them will cause the individual student to tighten the very muscles he or she is supposed to loosen, and loosen those which are supposed to be tightened. For this reason, some singing teachers in the United States instruct a student to imagine a hole between the eyes and to conceive of the sound of his or her voice as a fountain of water flowing out the hole. A young singer might be told to hold his or her mouth as if there was a pear in it.

One 'cellist in the United States teaches entirely by metaphor. He asks the student to imagine that he or she is riding a motorcycle instead of playing a 'cello, or chopping wood, or sawing logs, or that the student is a piston engine. Singers who are told to imagine that the sound is actually coming not from their mouths, but from a space approximately one foot directly above their heads are dealing with a concept which is half myth and half metaphor. Many metaphorical statements merge into mythical ones.

There are two ways in which one may use such statements. Either the teacher has found through experience that directing a student's attention to the musculature involved will cause the student to do the wrong thing, or a decision has been made that teaching is a mystical statement. This implies that it is impossible to teach anyone directly because the learning process involves such qualities as "talent" and the approach to divinity. This more mystical attitude, while useful in the understanding of great talent, probably has its roots in the culture.

Another common method throughout the world is teaching by rote. In this method, with or without the use of a notational system, students are asked to play something which might be called non-music, such as the Dastgah exercises of Persia or the scale patterns taught to classical music students in the European tradition. Here, what is learned and memorized is pre-music -- a series of study devices -- meaningless, musically, but they produce flexibility. Once learned, such devices are frequently used to warm the hands or voice before performing. The method of learning by rote is often exceedingly boring to the student, and seems to work better with older students than the younger ones. Older students can understand why they must go through these physical exercises such as lying on the floor and allowing someone to stand upon one's stomach; lifting weights; jogging; or doing some other physical exercises which seem totally un-musical.

An extremely common teaching method throughout the world is what Europeans and Americans call "coaching". In this style of teaching, an assumption is made that the individual already knows a piece of music fairly well. The business of the teacher/coach is to comment on nuances, rather than basic design.

Hours of discussion are spent over nuances in Maltese singing. The proper way of approaching a subject is hashed over afterwards and, if the singer is an apprentice, his teacher usually talks about the lofty ideals of singing, the responsibilities of genius and the beauty of proper expression. In this way, young men learn not only what is an acceptable verse, but what is an exceptional one. Famous verses of other singers are remembered for many years and often quoted as examples of the fine turning of a phrase. In American society, coaching is reserved for that period in time when a piece has been thoroughly learned but requires finishing touches.

Many styles involve learning without a teacher. Many individuals do their learning through listening to live music, television, radio, records, tapes and compact discs. The desire to learn may be so great that the individual who is isolated from established learning by one situation or another will turn to this method. Jazz musicians frequently learn their styles from intensive listening as teenagers. Shamans among the Kutenai have a body of liturgical songs which they must learn to perform properly. As there are no teachers, they must simply go from one shaman to another, learning their trade. The authors once observed a young banjo player teach himself. He sold flowers on the same street corner all day, every day, performing on the banjo as he waited for customers. As the year progressed, he grew more and more accomplished.

Finally, mention must be made of learning with a supernatural teacher. This is possibly a metaphor of some kind. Among the Central and Southern Sakalava and Vezo of Madagascar, the *salegy* or case zither is believed to be the instrument of the dead. Dead persons, especially nobility, are said to desire to hear or play the *salegy*. An individual may find him/herself seized with the desire to learn to play and is thought to be possessed by the spirit of a dead nobleman who wishes to perform. All *salegy* players agree that the teacher was the dead individual who possessed them and made their fingers move upon the strings. The burden of this type of performance is that the individual may be asked to play at any time, for everyone who is seized with the desire to hear *salegy* playing is also possessed by the spirit of the dead.

The most important example of learning from a supernatural teacher is the Vision Quest of the Plains Indians of North America. Young men who venture on the Vision Quest expect to see the spirit of a particular animal, plant or object which will give them special powers, including songs. Isolated from the rest of their society, hungry, often thirsty, frequently tired, these young men experience visions in which spirits come to them and teach them songs said to have specific powers. The young men are taught more than songs; they are often given the meanings behind the songs and shown how to apply them to specific situations. For example, some of these special songs are believed to have the power to draw game, if sung correctly in the proper context.

Another slightly more complex form of learning from the supernatural is the situation found among the Cherokee, where music has a special power. Life situations are countered among the Cherokee by the use of ritual formulae; any formula can be thought, whispered, spoken or sung. Singing is the most powerful usage. Those who perform ritual formulae say that there is a particular kind of singing which is correct or proper, called the "straight voice". A song sung with the "straight voice" is one in which the quality of the voice carries directly to the spirit for whom it is intended. This is obviously a metaphor and not a comment on voice type; "correct" singing is verified at least partly by the results, for if the correct results occur, then through time, the specialist learns which performance technique is regarded as correct by the spirits.

As can be seen above, music is learned by a number of different methods. It should also be apparent that the statements about learning are, in fact, cultural statements about music and not statements about learning. The method a culture chooses to pass on its musical traditions is predicated as much on cultural beliefs as upon musical exigency.

This is undoubtedly one of the most difficult aspects for the understanding of the acquisition of musical techniques, since two levels of understanding are dealt with within the same conceptual package.

What does a Cherokee diviner mean when he or she says someone has a "straight voice"? Do the Sakalava really learn to play the *salegy* from the spirits of the dead or do they learn the style from listening to other *salegy* players? Are we cheating certain of our talented young people through our teaching method and its visual implications?

All of these aspects of the questions of both teaching and learning move to the heart of the problem of ethnomusicology: the variety of human experience. Without multiple examples of learning procedures, understanding of the process will not soon be achieved. Each example, however, is rife with cultural implications and the ultimate necessity will be to extract from all these learning procedures the principles which will apply to the process, itself, if that is possible. As yet, the study of learning techniques is in its infancy. This is an area which is well worth stressing for future students in the field.

HOW COMPOSERS LEARN

In many societies, the composer is not different from the performer. This is particularly true in those societies where improvised music is more frequently found. There are numerous cases, however, where the composer is not always his or her own performer, or where not all performers are composers.

In Tikopia, the composer is known as the *purotu*, or

"expert". This is an individual who has been creating new songs of his own volition and whose songs have been judged to be good. Such a man is frequently called upon to create new songs for special occasions, such as a district or clan *feasinga* or *anga* feast for a privilege ceremonial. After consideration of the song to be created, he will ask for a rehearsal and will teach the singers the new song by the agonizing process of slowly repeating each syllable, with the singers following after him until they have caught both words and music. These practice sessions last for several hours; at the end of which time, the song is up to speed and the dancers are beginning to move to it. Thus, even in the simplest community, specialized composers are to be found.

This is an important point. Once again, the myth that "primitive" peoples have simpler music and simpler forms of composition, performance and audience response than one's own, is open to question. Throughout the world, composers exist at all levels. In some societies, they are named and their talents proclaimed. In others, each individual is a composer if he or she is a performer and if no one else repeats what he or she has done. In yet other societies, composers are innovators of new styles rather than of set pieces. This is true of guitar music in Malta where each piece is an improvised entity, but where three styles of guitar playing have developed in the general century, each due to a different man who is known as the father of the style. His innovations have been accepted; he cannot be personally imitated since the music is improvised; but his style can be copied.

The subject of composers is much more complex on a certain level than that of performers, since it implies something which may or may not be true elsewhere. The concept of the creator of music is one of the most difficult to handle well. Again, cultural impositions make it difficult to discuss composers as a whole. In some societies, such as the Hopi, no new compositions were produced for some time. The liturgical repertoire was set (Black, personal communication). In others, the dead, or spirits of the gods themselves, are the composers.

In societies where improvised music is the norm, creativity is the realm of the performer. As Herzog has put it:

> For us, it is an obvious matter to think of a piece of music apart from its performance; for a traditional singer, it is just as obvious that there is little, if any, existence to a song apart from its performance (Herzog, 1940:74).

Herzog states that the creative process precedes in time the performance which "merely reproduces" what has been fixed into a form. There is room for individual creation in traditional music, he says, but that the creative process consists mostly of re-creating and re-molding the music as it is being performed.

This re-molding process is an example of what folklorists regard as versions. There is no actual tale or narrative; rather, there are versions from which an ideal can be drawn.

This is also true of music. Who, then, is the composer? While one person may have created a particular piece of music initially, each performer or set of performers frequently changes it in the process. In these terms, they are adding to or subtracting from the initial plan. Thus, it is not the isolated composer who, like the Tikopia *purotu* (a specialist), creates his music beforehand, but rather that whole range of people who have to do with the process called "creativity" and who, whether called composers or performers, are part of the creative process in music.

This view immediately creates a composite model of the nature of creativity which is very different from the usual Euro-American view. The question is: What is creativity in man?

Creativity is to be distinguished from discovery in that discovery is the verbalization or revelation of something which is already *there*, such as gravity. The term, creativity, is usually reserved for those instances where mankind has taken upon itself the task of bringing something entirely new into the world. In these terms, the harnessing of fire by early man was not a creative act, but the cutting of certain stones to form tools *was*. The use of the principles of cross-breeding to produce different coat colors in horses is a discovery. Taken in this meaning, there have been few truly creative acts.

In these terms, is the "creation" of music a "creative" act? It occurs frequently and does not involve bringing something new into the world, so it is not "creative"; neither has it yet been demonstrated that music involves a discovery of natural principles. Another term, innovation, is reserved for this. The distinction between creation and innovation is that, while a creative act produces or manifests something totally new, an innovative one works within a set model to produce a variant of something already in existence. Thus, anyone who writes within the sonata form is producing or innovating another sonata within the same style.

70

In the same way, a person who makes a pot of soup, writes a sonnet, or composes a political speech is putting together items or ideas within a context of traditional form to produce a variant example of that form. The techniques in a particular form are probably similar; the individual item was created within a cultural style.

In music, this is most easily seen in improvised music; it must be extended cognitively to include other styles. Whether there are set pieces or improvisations, there are limits as to what new material is acceptable or expected. Items which fall outside the limits of style do not generally tend to be repeated; through loss of currency within a musical tradition, they are lost entirely.

Once again, the authors are maintaining that culture is the basic limiting context for music. Culture sets the following limitations upon music. First, basic trends represent types of music which are found to be acceptable within the framework of culture. Those items of performance which do not conform sufficiently to the basic trends usually are not repeated, and thus do not influence future events.

Second, the culture determines who may be a creator or innovator of music, whether tightly or loosely fashioned. At one point in history, it was acceptable for members of the Western upper class to indulge in the writing of music. In more recent times, however, very few upper class Europeans find this an acceptable mode of existence. In more traditional societies, the performance of music and the creation or the innovation of new elements within the style, have been tightly controlled by such devices as the restriction of music to particular lineages, clans, political groups or specific economic strata.

Third, cultural limitations are placed upon those creations which will survive. Ritualized music tends to last longer than secular, partly because certain pieces of music or styles of performance are designated as proper to given, highly structured moments of time and place. More secularized items may fall into complete disuse in the same time period by being replaced by either other examples of the same style, or other styles.

Fourth and finally, one who creates music will probably never be completely free, for his or her position in society is usually determined. Status forces the creator into certain poses which cannot be avoided without the danger of rejection from within the musical performing group. For example, when the improvisations of Indri Brincat, the foremost Maltese guitarist, became too abstruse and complex for his musical colleagues, he was simply no longer invited to play, although guitarists were in great demand. Complaints about his playing being non-traditional finally led him to the decision that he must revert to less daring improvisations as long as he continued to play in groups.

Thus, composers, also, learn their place within society and the limitations within which they may innovate; the styles within which they will be allowed to produce acceptable versions. Pressures are placed on all of the aspects of music -- listening, performing and composing. Because of the overwhelming influence of culture as context, almost no musical items can be said to be completely new or different.

FICTIVE STATEMENTS ABOUT MUSIC

Since music operates within the context of culture, a number of statements must be made which are presumptive of conformity to cultural ideals. In the broadest sense, it is these presumptive statements and their patterned results which are studied by ethnomusicologists. Many of these statements may be regarded as pure fiction; others, as superstition. Still others take the form of pure myths, being long narrative tales in which support for present action is placed into supernatural realms.

This collection of information is called "fictive statements" in order to include a number of different kinds of material which, on the surface, may seem to have little or nothing to do with one another. They all represent accepted ways of governing the process of musical expression within standard lines. Such items may be of several orders, depending upon the type of music and upon the nature of a particular cultural set of beliefs about music. In essence, these are beliefs which may or may not be acted upon, but which will have wide influence on performers, composers and listeners.

Most types of statements are negative validations of some kind and represent limiting factors; thus, they are the statement of context, ranging from simple terms of conversation to full stories. Primarily, they are statements involved in the learning of roles and then of re-creating an ascribed status or achieving a new status called musician. They are reflective of other contexts, the primary one being culture, itself.

The type of myth involved depends entirely upon the context of the music. For example, the Vision Quest seeks to acquire music as power. For the Cherokee, the singing of ritual chants adds special power to the chants; the context in which music is performed is that of spiritual or supernatural power. The purpose is to call spirits to the aid of man in the performance of certain duties which places a real proscription upon both those who sing and those who hear. The status involved is not so much that of musician, as of holder of spiritual power.

The role of musician involves several concomitants. The broadest is that of relationship of the musician to the society in which he or she lives. This is frequently explained in semi-musical statements; i.e., it is still common in New Orleans for jazz musicians to believe that the performance of any variety of secular music, and particularly jazz, invites eternal damnation. Jazz musicians are frequently shunned by good church-going people outside the context of musical performances; preachers denounce jazz from the pulpit, calling it the work of the Devil.

The Devil is unusually active in this syndrome because of the general association of Satan with stringed instruments and, particularly, with the guitar. Jazz performers still declare that it is the Devil who tempts them to play the guitar. The old European myth, taken from the older assumption that it is the Devil who teaches the violin, has marked jazz musicians in New Orleans as "different" from the average individual.

In a related semi-musical statement, both authors were told that musically talented young Southern ladies should not be trained to become professional musicians; their training should allow them to play the piano or sing only for company on Sunday afternoons or at teas. While many adventuresome and forthright young Southern ladies have calmly ignored this cultural proscription, it is an old one, nevertheless.

There has long been an association in the minds of Europeans between the need to acquire knowledge of the fine arts and something called "sophistication" or "culture". The educated young man or woman should be able to recognize Beethoven or Reubens, converse intelligently about the books of Meredith, and know a smattering of philosophy; it is not their place in life to write music, paint pictures, or write books. Any member of the upper class must take the fine arts lightly, and young Southern ladies are no exception. Musical accomplishment is perfectly correct; musical professionalism is not.

The relative status of a professional musician within the profession, especially that of a soloist, is predicated on other fictive statements. For Americans before World War II, there was the fictive statement of "arrival". The opera singer or concert artist of American descent who did not go to Europe on a tour was not considered to have "arrived", although this phenomenon seems to have broken down somewhat. Grace Brumbry, however, was ignored until she had visited European opera theaters. After this, her invitation to sing at the Kennedy White House assured her American career.

Similarly, to some Americans an opera singer is not regarded as having "arrived" until he or she has sung at the Metropolitan Opera House. The best example of recent years is Beverly Sills who was not invited to sing at the Metropolitan until late in her career and only came into national prominence with the publicity surrounding her late Metropolitan "debut".

Role and status are supported and controlled by fictive statements about the nature of "proper" behavior, "professional" achievement and general life condition. Musicians throughout the world are forced into roles which relate to their status as musicians.

In Malta, in order to be a musician one must not only be a genius, but also must bear the stigma of a fighter. It is assumed by those who do not sing that all singers, regardless of their singing style, are irascible fighting men. So firmly is this believed that bars must get a license from the police for singing performances, must stop all singing at 11 o'clock in the evening and are patrolled by the police for that time period.

This is undoubtedly the reflection of the *spirtu pront* (mentioned before) in which two men attempt to insult one another so cleverly that each is not offended by the insults. The proverbial and metaphorical statements used in such singing are of such value that it is a literary exercise rather than a pugilistic one. Nevertheless, singers are regarded as having bad tempers and he who would sing must bear the stigma.

The fictive statements concerning music may involve the questions of ownership or rights to music. This is an area where a clear-headed examination of the facts is necessary, since one believes so firmly in the fictive statements concerning music. Music is essentially ephemeral. It is performed; it disturbs the air and dies away. Attempts to put music into notation give only a partial imitation of what actually happens within a performance.

So, the question of the ownership of a song or of right to sing, specified under law or custom, becomes difficult to enforce. According to American ASCAP rules, anyone performing a song copyrighted by a particular composer must pay him or her a fee for the privilege. In fact, it is impossible to completely monitor the performing of music in American society or any other.

In some societies, ownership of music is regarded as absolute and supported by supernatural sanctions. Among certain Plains Indian tribes, only one man may sing a specific song and is generally the person who has received it during his Vision Quest from a spirit. For Northwest Coast Indians, songs may be transferred to others through inheritance; but supernatural sanctions occur when a song is sung by someone to whom it does not belong. This contrasts with the situation among the Merina of Madagascar, who have songs which are in the public domain. Anyone may sing them at any time. In Tikopia, music is recognized by special titles, but once a song is launched, anyone may change it.

In Malta, songs called *fatt* are individually created by singers of that style. Such songs are usually long, running sixty verses or more and requiring about half an hour to perform. The words are sometimes published in broadside sheets and sold on the streets although theoretically, only the composer, himself, should sing the song. If it is popular, however, others may choose to sing it as well.

During their first field investigation in Malta, the authors heard a somewhat changed version of a well-known song by the *fatt* composer, Joseph Fenech. Upon query about what should have been done, Mr. Fenech said he did not know his song had been revised by a younger singer; that such action was all right, but that the young man should have acknowledged him as the original composer and asked his permission as a matter of courtesy.

Here are a number of examples of different ideas about ownership of music -- all supported either by supernatural sanctions or simple recognition. Some societies mention the name of the composer; some do not. In each case, there are statements about what should have been done concerning ownership.

Rights are similarly differentiated from one society to another and the right to perform a piece of music varies widely. Among the Plains Indians and among the Kwakiutl of the Northwest Coast, no one has the right to perform a song except the owner or inheritor. The Kwakiutl owner has absolute right to perform the song, although he may choose to give it away in a potlatch. The right to perform songs is similarly controlled in Western society through the fiction of copyright; as mentioned above, a fee should be paid if a song is to be performed.

In some cases, the right to perform a particular piece of music is controlled by religious sanctions wherein certain religious music is only performable by priests or shamans. The revolt of Martin Luther was a shocking shift in cultural emphasis, with one of its most potent revelations the thought that lay persons might have free access to the Bible and could sing hymns. Catholics were similarly outraged by the idea of the Black Mass, in which the Mass is performed backwards. The right to perform may be controlled by fictive statements as well and in the Inquisition, such statements were backed up by negative sanctions.

The use of time and place as limiting factors upon the performance of music might also be included in the concept of fictive statements. Certain types of songs are performed only in seasonal feasts, festivals in their proper position, or at specific moments. The concept of proper time and place for the performance of particular pieces of music is frequently supported by true myth, as in the case of religious ritual.

In the Work of the Gods of Tikopia, the ownership, privilege of performance and proper time of performance are all tightly controlled. Many songs have accompanying myths indicating why they are sung in their present position in rites. At the other end of the scale, secular music in Tikopia is similarly controlled as to time and place, but by more prosaic means. In the evening *mako* or dance, when young people get together for a pleasant evening of entertainment and recreation, songs called *tauangutu* and *feuku* are sung only after all married people have left the grounds. As these songs are of a derisive sexual nature, it is felt improper to sing them before one's mother's family or in-laws. As this includes only married people in this instance, the implication is that the young wait until authoritarian figures have left the field before using dirty words.

There are a great number of fictive statements concerning performance. These are usually taught either by a specific teacher or, in ritual circumstances, by fictive statements which support the assumption of rightness or properness for particular styles. For Western cultures, the minor mode is usually regarded as proper to sad music; for Arabic cultures, the reverse is the case. Therefore, certain associations grow up between musical style or type of mode and type of feelings. This is the broadest possible context for such fictive statements.

Other such statements which may seem familiar are, "You cannot play the Bach Unaccompanied Suites in public until you have practiced them for at least six years". These Unaccompanied Suites for 'cello are not, for the most part, sufficiently difficult to require six years of practice, yet young 'cellists are frequently told that these simple pieces are difficult, so that as a result, they have great trouble interpreting them properly. Here is a case in which a fictive statement has been introduced to change behavior in that what was easy has become difficult.

In certain popular music circles, it is felt appropriate to say that one cannot play particular kinds of music well "unless one is stoned". As a result, aspiring musicians frequently feel that they must smoke marijuana or take stronger drugs for musical inspiration; however, the source for this fictive statement may well be that particularly able musical innovators have so many demands for performance that they feel they have to resort to drugs in order to continue to meet incessant concert or recording pressures. Whatever the source of this statement, this approach clearly changes behavior.

Although the locus and intensity of fictive statements vary widely, depending on the society or sub-group being investigated, it is of considerable value to the researcher. Proscriptive statements of this variety tend to indicate more clearly than do instructional procedures how one is to approach a particular style.

Perhaps the most interesting area in which fictive statements are used has to do with instruments. As King has mentioned (1976), musical instruments are not only objects, but are also cultural objects which live a life of their own. For example, European stringed instruments have many of the characteristics of human beings: they have necks, heads, bellies, backs and ribs. They are said to live and die and to have the need to breathe in humid weather. They are believed to be able to catch cold -- probably in reference to a shift in tone color. Older instruments are described as getting tired. Certain instruments made by the Amati family, for instance, are now regarded as "too tired" to be played in public.

The French violin maker, Villaume, attempted to improve the tone of his instruments by carving out a thinner space inside the belly (some storytellers say that he carved the thinner portion on the cheeks of the instruments, i.e., that portion above the f-holes on the front) in order to make them more responsive. All of these instruments are said to sound beautifully, but to tire quickly so that after half an hour, the sound is gone.

Fictive statements of this kind concerning musical instruments occur in almost all societies, whether the instruments are used for sacred or secular purposes. The individuality of sound of particular instruments, or the peculiarities of the wood or metal used excite comment. Such comments tend to fall into categories, although they will vary from culture to culture. While Europeans seem to believe that their instruments are partially alive and partially human, other societies may have a different concept. These are metaphorical statements, but the fact that they fall into a pattern indicates an underlying basic belief system. These are more than simply metaphors; they represent an attempt to make an object into a cultural object with qualities ascribed to it according to whatever principle is at work in the society in question.

Ownership of instruments is often an easy way to understand the fictive statements about them. In Western society, rare stringed instruments are not regarded as owned; they are historical objects, on loan for the lifetime of the performer. This concept places some distance between the performer and the instrument upon which he or she performs and gives performers a certain level of respect for the instrument. Musicians would tend to agree that it is difficult to own an instrument created before they were born, which will undoubtedly be in use after they are dead. The sense of continuity is given reality by the fictive statement.

In spite of the fact that they are bought and paid for, some instruments can never be truly owned. The sacred drums of the Buganda are the property of the king, or more properly, of kingship, for the drum-makers and their performers are employed by the king. The drums, themselves, are regarded as sacred and have their own houses in which to live. Among the Betsileo, tube zithers are highly personalized objects. In order to make them perform better, they are covered with amulets of various kinds to ensure that the person who plays them will be adept. Such instruments do not pass from hand to hand. They are not for sale; each musician must make his own. Old instruments belonging to someone now dead are regarded as having lost interest in the world, themselves. They, too, are semi-human after the death of the owner.

In some societies, the right to own and play an instrument is determined by desire, as in Western society and among the Central Sakalava. In others, musical instruments are a mark of the distinction between one style and another in the sense that only those who have the right to perform a particular style may own the requisite instrument and play it. Instruments frequently partake of the basic ethos that lies behind the style.

Among the Bara of Madagascar, the musical bow is an instrument devoted to magic, used to accompany songs by which the singer tries to force new patterns of activity on the world about him. When a man is drafted into the Army against his wishes, for instance, he visits the desert with a musical bow, playing and singing the same song repeatedly. The words of the song are designed to stop him from being drafted. Or, a Bara being forced into marriage may sneak off into the desert with his musical bow, trying to forestall the marriage. The bow is believed to bear the message to friendly spirits who will hear one's plea and correct the situation. While musical bows are easy enough to make, their association with magic precludes their being used for anything else.

The viol, on the other hand, is the primary instrument associated with *bilo*, that variety of possession in which an individual is either made sick by evil spirits or is forced to dance with them. Once the condition has been diagnosed, viol players are called and asked to play for the sick person until the spirit has been driven out of the body, either by recovery or through exaggerated dancing. The music of the viol and its association with *bilo* means that the instrument, itself, is a restricted object and cannot be used for the singing of love songs, minor magic or sagas.

The pattern of relationship between musical instruments and cultural ethos is also found in the concept of "breaking in". New instruments in Western society are believed to be inadequate to their task. It is said, for instance, that it requires fifteen years of playing to "break in" a Steinway grand piano. Stringed instruments are regarded as similarly unresponsive; during the first ten to twelve years of their effective life, their tone quality is considered faulty. This is the motive which lay behind Villaume's attempt to create an instrument with thinner cheeks, for he was attempting to reduce the breaking-in time. This concept fits well with the idea that no individual owns an instrument. Fifteen years is a long time in the life of a professional performer; to waste it on a *new* instrument is regarded as criminal.

It is interesting to note that only expensive instruments of our culture are regarded in this way -- a new flute, costing less than $1,000, is regarded as playable at once. The idea that extremely expensive instruments, such as grand pianos and stringed instruments, must be broken in and are therefore not worth making, is parallel to the present trend in Euro-America where the manufacture of fine instruments is declining. Given the present conditions in which a fine Stradivarius 'cello would now cost upwards of a quarter of a million dollars, one would think that players would be glad to have modern instruments. Whether this is the final playing out of the myth that no one owns an instrument or a single rationalization for the end of an era is unknown.

These few examples of the nature of fictive statements about music-learning, ownership, performance and instruments are exceedingly tentative, partly because this material is not well investigated throughout the world. However, there is enough information available to indicate that a wide range of statements about the nature of music and the proscriptions placed upon both instruments and performers exist.

What is significant about these statements is that they seem to be patterned in some way. It can be estimated that such statements represent some kind of basic ethos about music which is culturally defined and maintained. To know more about music, the recovery of such statements and their organization into the basic patterns is an area of investigation which might prove extremely fruitful. At this point in time, this is no more than a suggestion; but like all aspects of music study, it will take on a life of its own if those interested in studying music care to pursue it.

KINESICS

In previous sections, items of learning have been discussed which are perhaps more basic to correct perform-ance than is kinesics, the study of physical movement. Some physical movements are clearly related to the task of the performing of music, taught in fairly prosaic ways, having no undue verbal or metaphorical implications. Others are not; they seem mainly to be the end result of what might be called virtuosic embellishment.

Whatever the case may be, musicians generally move differently from other human beings, thus producing a visible impression for the observer. Musicians kinetically mark their social difference by physical movements, some of which are explicable by the requirements of the instrument they play; some are not.

This impression of virtuosic embellishment has been noted before by ethnographers working in other areas, particularly religion. In speaking of Polynesian religion, Lowie notes:

> ...We must not be hypnotized by the high-sounding concoctions of the native priests. These were specialists, and like all specialists, tended to become virtuosos, who ostentatiously exhibited their skill in handling and amplifying tradi-tional lore. A favorite device of

theirs was to picture the gradual unfolding of the world in successive generations marked by distinct entities ... Whether we regard this as profound wisdom or pretentious and meaningless verbiage, will depend on our metaphysical taste. But no one can seriously believe that anyone, the priesthood included, turned to such phraseology for a solution of life's problems (1937:304-305).

While some Polynesian specialists may cavil at Lowie's implication here, he has stated fairly well a major characteristic of all specialists: one of their tasks is to embroider upon basic designs.

While the playing of music obviously requires movement, there is no real need for that movement to be as stylized as it is; nor does playing the role of musician need to be as stylized. The fact that embellishments of behavior of this kind exist are interesting and sometimes useful.

What a musician does with his body might be described as a kind of dance. In the context of highly formalized behavior called music, musicians also formalize other aspects of their behavior. There is a wide range of possibility here; for example, brass sections in orchestras frequently use mutes which come in two varieties -- wooden or metal. One way of formalizing non-musical behavior is for the section leader or conductor to insist that all mutes in the section be made of the same material, be it wood or aluminum. As King has put it:

...When you formalize, what you are in effect saying for the audience, or the participation of the audience, is "this is our specialty, this is something that we do, and we are showing you this." In other words, "these are things that you do not find time to learn, or you do not have the circumstances to learn in our culture, so we will formalize this and show it to you"...I think that when you get to the point of performance there is formalization because the specialist -- who is the musical performer or the group of performers -- is signaling the whole audience that this is the way we communicate to you what we do and what you don't do (1976:231-232).

King is indicating a spillover from the formalization of music to the formalization of the behavior surrounding music. Herndon calls this "dancing":

...I've dispassionately watched a pianist dancing over a piano, or a 'cellist dancing over a 'cello with a special kind of ferocity which is totally unnecessary to technically performing a piece of music. It is stagecraft (op. cit.:232-233).

Some varieties of stagecraft of this kind are stylized and

87

conscious. When violinists bow together in ensembles, when brass sections all use the same kind of mute, when performers must all dress in the same kind of costume, one is dealing with conscious stagecraft.

Among the Betsileo, all players of *rija* (a variety of minstrelsy), wear sunglasses and berets. They consciously attempt to undermine class behavior by placing audiences in the position where persons of higher class must lower their heads below those of lower class in order to listen carefully to their music. They do this, generally, by scooting up to a wall of a bandstand instead of playing in an open space so that people in the first row, usually of higher class, must therefore lean down if they wish to see them. The *rija* player thus deliberately attempts to produce negative behavior on the part of the audience.

Jazz musicians may well be conscious of their aversion to contact with the audience, as mentioned earlier. In New Orleans at The Famous Door, the stage is actually inside the bartender's area; the bar is U-shaped with the musicians' raised stage behind the bar. The performers, all white, wear sunglasses or look at the ceiling in order to avoid eye contact with the audience.

A vast contrast is available just a half-block away at Preservation Hall, the major arena for old-time jazz in New Orleans, where the vast majority of the performers are black and over 60 years of age. In this hall there is no stage; performers are on the same floor level as the audience without a protective rail or any other device. When the chairs have been filled, the audience members sit on cushions directly in front of the musicians. Under normal performance circumstances, jazz is played here without any barrier between audience and performer, with the audience so close that those in the first rows can smell the breath and body sweat of the performers. During performance breaks, performers and audience mingle with no physical barriers exhibited by performers, who look directly at the people, allow themselves to be touched and converse freely with audience members.

This marked contrast between black and white jazz musicians in New Orleans is an indication of the kinesic and stagecraft styles of two different cultures approaching the same music. It is a startling contrast, particularly in view of the fact that the same people may be in both audiences on any given evening.

In Bali, performers are taught correct facial expressions as well as correct performance styles. Thus, cultures demonstrate in many kinesic ways that an individual is doing a performance and, since music is a performing art, it partakes of this quality.

The significance of kinesics has yet to be properly investigated. Such stagecraft and formalization of behavior is patterned and highly so. It is practically axiomatic in anthropology that wherever general behavior is so patterned, the culture is expressing something specific. In view of the fact that these formalized behaviors are associated directly with public performances where such symbolic cues are usually presented, it is practically incumbent on ethnomusicology to further investigate this little nown area.

The question of why a particular behavioral pattern occurs is difficult, if not impossible, to assess at the present time. It is easy enough for the authors to say for Malta that the reason performers keep such a wide space between them when singing is that they are performing an argument in public. Their gestures, lack of eye contact and physical distance are a play upon the normal conditions of two people who are having a serious argument. Of course, the musicians are not really arguing; they are acting out an argument.

This becomes even more significant when one realizes that, in Malta, the greatest fear is of *vendetta*, that condition in which an argument leads to total lack of social control except for violence. *Vendetta* can go on for generation after generation; the arguments of the fathers are visited upon the children. Property is destroyed; lives are lost or twisted by association with one or other sides of such a quarrel. Yet, it is this most feared element of culture which is acted out by singers of *spirtu pront*, the most popular of the singing and performing styles of Malta. Why?

One explanation lies in the old adage that people sing what they cannot say. People cannot talk about *vendetta* easily; their fears are suppressed. Maltese talk around the concept by various means, but it is only musicians who can freely discuss it. These are the knights-errant of Maltese culture, men strong enough and courageous enough to face the culture's greatest fear in public, by performing insults. Is this a general function of music? Is music the area in which a culture allays its anxiety? From the Maltese example, this seems to be an adequate explanation.

CONCLUSION

This chapter has been concerned with what is learned about music as well as how music is learned. An attempt has been made to indicate the way in which music is framed within a culture. Stress has been placed upon the ability of a culture to encapsulate experience, formalize it and control it through tradition.

Some of the means are the instruments chosen; how the performers are taught to play them; the styles which are obligatory; the way in which performers are taught; the way in which audiences react to music; the kind of talented individual which any given culture will accentuate or emphasize; and the variety of fictive statements which surround teaching. In addition, the fact that kinesic behavior, itself, falls into patterns which may be culturally relevant has been discussed.

The major emphasis has been on the traditional aspects of a supposedly creative act. Music does not occur within a vacuum; it lives within a set of values which shape and control it almost totally. So traditional are the attitudes toward music that its formalized nature is not surprising; what is surprising is that new pieces of music are continually being put forward.

It is within the context of high formalization and heavy cultural pattern that innovation in music occurs. Although there have been a multitude of writings on the importance of the innovative quality of music, the question must be asked whether the emphasis on music as a "creative act" may be the result of subliminal recognition that music is hardly a free good. If music is compared with language, for instance, it is found that any human being who can speak correct grammatical sentences is forever creating new ones. Yet, language is usually not thought of as a creative medium, unless it is written.

Viewed in this light, language is a highly creative art,

but a very common one. Music, on the other hand, usually occurs in repeated set pieces. What a musical performer does, essentially, is to repeat over and over the same musical sound. Consider the fine art tradition where the works of a Beethoven or a Bartok will be heard innumerable times within a single year. A new composition -- a new re-assembling of familiar sounds -- is an uncommon occurrence in music; yet it is called a creative art. Why?

It would appear from this that music has been mis-labeled. Music is not nearly so creative as language; in fact, it is highly redundant and formalized. Yet, it is frequently to this medium that one turns when one speaks of the highest goals or the finest hour of human beings. To emphasize once more the creative aspects of music would be only to reinforce our culture's view of it.

In those instances where no new pieces can be added to the repertoire, music is not a creative act at all. The learning procedures -- both formal and informal, musical and non-musical -- are highly stylized, even to the point of producing kinesics for performers when they are off-stage or not playing.

It would appear that this study is dealing with a variety of human behavior which is one of the most traditional and culture-bound in existence. Given the total range of human attitudes toward music, one would be tempted, at first, to say that there are traditional societies on the one hand and "fine art" societies on the other. These would be distinguished by a higher level of creativity in the "fine art" tradition, such as our own. Yet even here, major emphasis is not on the creation of the new, but on the reproduction of the tradition-al.

The only area in our musical repertoire where this is not true is in interpretative and improvisatory styles, such as jazz. In the area of popular songs which ordinarily would be called a mark of the traditional society, our own tradition is the most creatively active. It is here that new pieces are continually being added to the repertoire, not in the area of the fine arts.

Taken all together, the musical "creativity" of any culture is minimal in comparison with the ordinary conversation of a six-year-old child, when looked at as a creative art. There are an infinite number of sentences in any language. Are there an infinite number of pieces in any musical tradition? This discussion of one of the fine arts has stressed the non-creative and stereotyped aspect of it. Many will balk at this view; but after due consideration, some will ask the most significant question which this text attempts to put forward: What *is* music?

4

THE RELATIONSHIP OF MUSIC
TO
SOCIAL INSTITUTIONS

In this chapter, focus is placed on three areas of human life which impinge in a major way on music. Although these are not the only areas which may interact with the musical sphere, the interrelationship occurs sufficiently often cross-culturally to require special consideration. These areas are: economics, politics and religion.

The concept of music as economic or political may seem confusing at first, while the relationship between religion and music is more obvious. In each case, these are general cover concepts for kinds of actions that human beings do which can be grouped together and discussed in isolation from other aspects of human life. Like music, itself, each represents a way of viewing activity which is slightly different from the other. Although these cover terms are undoubtedly Western in origin, they are a means (but not the only one) of cross-cutting and categorizing human behavior.

In terms of a value set like music, economics, politics and religion are aspects of the theoretical view of life rather than hard facts. They are part of the superstructure of one's way of viewing the world rather than truly isolatable elements. The way in which economics interacts with music, for instance, is a variety of theoretical frameworks. These frameworks are mentioned here because they are so frequent in the study of music, that students may be predisposed to consider one of these aspects of the theoretical approach to human life as a reasonable field of study adjunct to the study of ethnomusicology.

ECONOMICS

Economics as a concept may be helpful in the study of ethnomusicology in that it masses together certain data concerning musicians which can easily be ignored. Concentration upon performance, style, learning, or analysis of music omits account of the ways in which musicians use their music as an economic good or a status good, and the more pragmatic gains (or losses) involved in music-making.

From the point of view of the musicians, music-making may be a way of social interacting, of economic gain, or of achieving a comfortable status if a musician's status is not ascribed. From the point of view of society, the musician may fall into normal social categories and thus fit into the economic system in a particular way. As Merriam stated it:

> Such acknowledgement may be forthcoming in a number of ways. The most visible, of course, is payment -- either in the form of the abstraction of wealth repre-

sented by money tokens, or in the form of basic economic goods -- which, if sufficient to support the musician totally, acknowledges complete professionalism. "Payment" may also be in the form of gifts given to the performer, in which case total economic support may not be forthcoming; and in some societies, the musician's contribution may be acknowledged only by the recognition of ability unaccompanied by any form of emolument (op. cit., 125).

It has been pointed out for Madagascar (McLeod, 1964) that craft specialization is a more complex factor even than this. If the specialist is, as Herskovits has stated, he who carries on a given craft (1950:273), with the implication that those who have knowledge of a skill are specialists, the situation becomes confusing since, in Madagascar, there are more people who play, sing and dance than there are people regarded as specialists. There, the recognition of the specialist by the community is clear with three criteria for distinction: (1) music regarded as necessary for certain occasions will be performed only by specialists; (2) such specialists in contradistinction to other musicians will receive gifts for their performances, whether adequate to support them or not; and (3) such musicians will, as a result, carry a definable status in the community in question (McLeod, 1964:278-279).

Distinction is made here between music designed for special purposes, carried by specialists as defined above, and music for other purposes carried by non-specialists. This somewhat confusing situation is more characteristic of economics without money than those with money. Western society, wherein the profit motive is supreme and status is defined in terms of money, is somewhat easier to handle in this respect.

Those societies which are partially in the money economy contain elements of social divisions of labor which are differentially rewarded. In Madagascar, there are musical specialists upon whom attention is focused and there are musical persons upon whom no attention is focused. Because of other situations, it is not always the specialists who perform the ritual music in ritual circumstances.

For instance, among the Central Sakalava, the musical specialist is paid to perform the role of diverting the attention of evil spirits from rituals, while other musicians are actually performing the ritual. This division of labor is understandable in view of the Malagasy concept of the supernatural as peopled by ancestors, gods and spirits who are sometimes antipathetic to human life and who will seek at certain points in life history to interfere with the activities of men. While specialists divert the inimicable spirits, non-specialists are invoking the benevolent. Who, then, is the musical specialist? In this case, the presence of payment marks not specialism, but a particular kind of activity. The division goes even further; those who are paid to perform are called musicians, while those who are actually performing vital rituals in the midst of musical "noise" are regarded not as making music, but as entertaining themselves.

The question of social acceptance of a person as a musician is a vexed one. The musician may be a professional in that most of his or her income is derived from the performance of a skill. The musician may be a specialist, in that he or she is recognized as the proper person to perform certain types of music, receiving some kind of gift for it. Or, he or she may be a skilled performer of types of music for which either no payment is involved or there is no social recognition as a musician.

William P. Malm recounted a case in point. A man was standing in the middle of his field playing a flute. An onlooker, when asked what the man was doing, replied that he was farming. Thus, there can be varieties of music occurring which are carried by skilled performers, complex in nature and highly stylized, but which are regarded as a kind of activity other than music. Thus, the American profit-oriented view of professionalism and its ramifications may not always help in finding out what is happening.

On the whole, it is easier to see professionals or specialists at work because their activities are marked in some way. This does not imply that the reasons for marking their behavior are musical ones or even economic ones. For an overview of such information as is now available on the general implications of the social status of musicians who are recognized as specialists, see Merriam (1964), McLeod (1964), and Ames (1973).

The least difficult area for the ethnomusicologist to deal with concerns ways of acknowledgement of the musical specialist -- gifts or other payment, and the holding of some identifiable status. Payment can be defined and the relative income or status from musicianly activities measured. Attitudes toward one's musicianship can similarly be defined, but present greater difficulties.

Ames points out that, when asked what they did for a living, musicians among the Igbo of Obimo usually identified themselves as farmers. In contrast, Hausa musicians from Zaria regarded music as an occupation and a source of livelihood, yet both receive some payment for their musical activity. The stress laid upon such return was more significant among Hausa musicians than Ibgo; this distinction is both between cultures and between an urban and a rural setting.

It is more common in rural settings for persons skilled in the craft of music to identify themselves as something other than musicians. Multiple roles are, of course, more common in rural than in urban societies and this may be a mark of this distinction.

Almost no information is available concerning actual payment for musical activities. In those societies where a money economy is not present (few as they are), livelihood is not determined by the possession of cash or goods. Communities at this level tend to work together for a common goal -- usually survival -- and, if possible, no one goes hungry.

In Tikopia, one of the few societies viewed by anthropologists before the introduction of a money economy, musical specialists are rewarded in the same way as others. Here, gifts of bark-cloth called *ufi* are ceremoniously exchanged in public to mark the honor done by the presentation of a ritual, a song, the presence of family at a funeral or wedding and so forth. The bark-cloth cannot be regarded as payment for services, since it is immediately exchanged for another bark-cloth of similar quality. Instead, honor is conferred by this variety of gift-exchange, a practice common among Malayo-Polynesian peoples (Firth, 1939:229).

Madagascar is also a culture heavily influenced by the Malayo-Polynesian tradition and, as a whole, is a gift-exchange area where allegiances, relationships, honors, kindnesses and economic transactions all depend upon an equal return for every social gesture. A musician, living in a tit-for-tat world, can expect to be repaid for his services in some way. Madagascar has entered into the money economy and for these reasons, two types of exchange take place in every transaction. Fees are frequently set by specialists for performances in public in the tradition of the money economy, with rates varying according to type of music to be played.

Additionally, an elaborate set of exchanges which enhance and honor a transaction exists. When the listeners are happy with a performer who was given a set fee, they will give him something extra. This concept, called *cadoa* (Fr., cadeau), is identical to the French concept of *lagniappe* (and may even derive from it); an additional fillip to the delicacy of social interaction. When a *cadoa* is given, the musician will often reciprocate in the form of another song. Another *cadoa* will bring forth yet another song until listeners and performers, alike, feel that a social bond has been cemented. Where the relationship is not a one-to-one confrontation, elaborations of this kind cannot happen.

The set fee is an indication of the presence of the money economy; the *cadoa* is a remnant of the older gift-exchange principle. In rural areas of Madagascar, musicians are usually paid with food; again, in ritual situations, individual musicians receive a set amount. In the less highly patterned situations, the concept of exchange is present; whether the gift be money or food, the interchange is both economic and social. It may be stretching a point to call this "payment", but here, music itself is regarded as something which can be given as a gift for which an equal gift may be received in return.

Ames points out another situation among the Hausa, where professional singers sing the praises of individuals and almost demand gifts in return:

> The musicians themselves tend to have a commercial attitude toward their craft, viewing it simply as the means for earning a living. This craft mentality is quite evident in the typical behavior of the musician. It is reflected in his habit of scheduling annual tours through the countryside just after the cash crop has been marketed, and in his practice of consulting musicians when on tour, in order to learn who, among the wealthy, are likely to be generous givers (1973-:265).

The Hausa singers tend to urge generous giving on the part of those for whom they sing and, if not satisfied, may shame the giver in song.

The Igbo musicians of Obimo also receive gifts, but with a completely different attitude of prizing the gifts, not for monetary value, but for the giving of them. The Obimo are also not as likely to shame stingy persons in song.

Among the Maltese folk musicians, there is also a distinction based on pay. The singers of *spirtu pront*, the song duel, frequently perform at different kinds of functions, and a few make commercial recordings; however, only those who are regarded as truly skilled are paid for their efforts. A fine musician often has followers among the audience, who especially enjoy his improvisations and who may ask him to assemble a group to perform on a specific occasion for the standard fee of one pound per man for a single performance. The normal number of performers is seven -- four singers forming two separate song duels, plus three guitarists. In addition to the more formal fee, the Maltese sometimes give a gift of food to performers; after the legal hour of 11:00 p.m. has passed, singers and guitarists may be invited to partake of a dinner. This latter is more a gift than a payment for the giving of food in Malta has social overtones; it expresses friendship, intimacy and appreciation.

The Maltese musician, sufficiently skilled to be paid for his performance, cannot earn his living from music alone, but uses the performing of music as a way of creating extra income. Many musicians make their living through what Levi-Strauss has called *bricolage*, that economic process called "jack of all trades". The *bricoleur* of Malta may be a farmer who supplements his income by any number of other things, music among them. Musicians tend to view music simultaneously as great art, fine entertainment and a potential source of income; but this attitude is as true of hunting or wine-making as it is of music.

The illustrations given of the way in which music is economically advantageous in certain societies tend to strengthen the impression that the general economic situation will influence music in some way. The presence of gift exchange in Madagascar allows music to be an acceptable gift in certain circumstances; the praise songs of Hausa musicians are regarded as an economic intangible good; in Malta, music is one of the possible ways a man may earn a little extra money.

The fact that various economic systems place different emphasis on musical styles or performers is an indication of the reasons for the difficulty in understanding musical specialists. In Malta with its profit motive, the situation is clear: if a musician is not good enough to be paid, he will not be. In Madagascar, skilled people cannot be paid for some of their musical services, because to do so would call attention to them and thus defeat the purpose for which they are singing. In the one case, the unpaid musician is not as skilled; in the other, he is equally skilled, so there is no necessary relationship between skill and payment. This implies that there may be specialists who do what they do musically for reasons that are not monetary. It would, therefore, appear unwise at this time to equate the concepts of skill and specialism until further information on the role of economic systems in musical production is ascertained.

In a broader sense, economics in the sense of *exchange* is a useful concept in respect to music. In most societies, there is usually some system of exchange which is important. It may be monetary, as in profit-oriented societies; it may be ceremonial or may denote rank and kinship. Exchange may be a general means of gluing a system together and as such, exchange is one of the grouping mechanisms of human culture. Malinowski has emphasized the concept of commensality -- eating together -- as a highly functional way of cementing social relations between people.

Music, like every other variety of human behavior, may have its place as a means of demonstrating the importance of a given occasion. When a group sits down to a wedding breakfast, music may be necessary to mark it as special. Performances to mark ceremonial points in life are common; but many societies use music as a social glue of some kind. In each society, occasions where music is publicly performed usually indicate the necessity to express -- and thereby relieve -- social tensions.

The *feasinga*, large daytime recreational performances of Tikopia, are a means for bringing together contrasting social groups who represent opposing social segments within the society. These are the clans, the districts of the island (between whom there is great variety) and various villages. Rivals come together at the *feasinga* to dance together, to exchange personnel in dances, to eat one another's food, thus symbolizing for a moment the relaxation of social tensions.

The all-pervasiveness of music may lie in its close association with the public expression of sentiment of one kind or another. Because music is so frequently accompanied by linguistic texts, statements can be made in public in a highly formalized way, thus giving public validity to certain sentiments which are privately not espoused. Performances, themselves, may be viewed as forms of economic exchange, or in a wider sense as social exchange. Here, people come together to express public sentiment and, by so doing, may publicly alleviate private quarrels or tensions momentarily.

POLITICS

The definition of politics is arguable in detail. However, all anthropologists agree on two major qualities of the political: (1) a political group coordinates behavior for its mutual defense; and (2) political behavior is definable as any means for the management of internal group aggression.

The politics of music has at least two levels: the politics of musicians' groups, whether or not they include the audience; and the wider role politics of music may play in the structure and functioning of a society. Nor should the potential role of music itself as a form of political expression be disregarded. This has been discussed by Betty Wang (1965) for China, where folk songs were used as an indicator of public opinion.

The question arises as to the position of politics and its relationship to a musicians' group. It should be remembered that in some societies, such as the Karimojong (Gourlay, 1972), everyone is a musician and there is no large classification called "music". In other societies, it is possible that musicians do not communicate to a great extent, although it is probable that in most societies, musicians' groups are formed at some level of tightness.

When a definite musical group is present, it may be possible to derive insights from a consideration of their processes and activities. The musical group may be viewed as a fairly clear-cut accessible entity, a functional organism having most, if not all, of the characteristics possessed by any society. In terms of particular societies, if human behavior may be expected to repeat itself on the micro- and macro-levels, music provides a convenient, almost universally acceptable area of focus for the study of an encapsulated structure, reflecting numerous other aspects of concern.

The study of politics with regard to musical groups

implies that such entities exist; thus, it is first necessary to know what a group is. In the study of social structure, the total configuration, interaction and articulation of groups, care must be taken to employ definitions which reflect analytical goals and purposes.

There are several kinds of general distinctions which may be made concerning the nature and identity of human groups. Contrast between territorial and special-purpose, kinship and non-familistic, voluntary and non-voluntary, or between volitional and ascribed membership in groups may be convenient, depending upon one's goals. Whatever one's specific interest may be, it is first necessary to examine carefully the more general kinds of relationships which identify musicians' groups *vis-a-vis* other groups.

Often, although not always, musicians' groups will be "voluntary" in nature rather than being based on kinship or residence. In Malta, there is a level of grouping which might be done on the basis of kinship; many of the sub-groups are residential while the larger entities are not. Membership in musicians' groups might be called "voluntary", although volition is not sufficient cause for admission to the group.

Maltese musicians have a practical necessity for grouping together because the song duel requires an opponent. It is difficult to discuss or debate with one's self for any period of time; it is not easy to sing without musical accompaniment, and most singers have a severely limited command of guitar techniques. On one level, the formation of groups may be seen to be the consequences of practical requirements.

In composition, Maltese musicians' groups are not necessarily territorial, although there is a tendency for grouping to occur according to village of origin. Any grouping by village of residence is usually restricted to what might be called village groups which are of secondary importance, both artistically and politically. Kinship ties, as well, are not a prerequisite to group formation; they do exist in many instances, but are not the sole compositional factor.

Maltese musicians' groups are not status-linked, age-grouped, or related to occupation, but are based on a series of variables and a conglomerate of possibilities which may result in temporary or permanent association of individuals -- an association for the purpose of interaction via the means of music and its related activities.

The authors would suggest that, after their experiences in Malta, the term "group" might be used as a generic referent to all types of linkages between musicians. In Malta, there are ideally two groups at any given time but, due to change, it is evident that three or more factions are in operation, although most musicians will insist that there are only two. Given a period of time, the situation may change so that there are only two factions.

Anthropologists comment that factional situations occur frequently. There are usually two factions in community organization (Linton, 1936:229). On the tiny island of Tikopia, there are two rivaling districts, Faea and Revenga; among the Hopi, there are the "hostile" and "friendly" factions; and Boissevain (1965, 1969) describes dualistic organizations for Malta.

Factions, whether two or more, commonly oppose one another in various activities and boast about their own superi-

107

ority. Murdoch (1949:90) suggests that ethnocentrism is a possible function of factionalism, which provides a sort of safety valve for the release of aggression.

Additionally, factions are not ever considered to be headed by non-officials (Clark, 1968:151). Throughout all the considerations of factionalism, however, the nature of it seems to have eluded definition, possibly due to the widespread existence of the phenomenon and the fact that it is often impossible to study both factions in a two-part situation. Perhaps the key to understanding the nature of factionalism lies in the concept of opposition. In the study of kinship-based systems, Smith (1956:39-80) and Sahlins (1961:332-345) have discussed the nature of segmentary opposition.

In Malta, factions are not kinship-based; nor may they be considered to be permanent organizations of opposition, although both segmentation and opposition seem to apply. Maltese factions seem to employ the concept of complementary opposition which involves the massing of equivalent segments in defense, exposition, or exploitation of privileges, rights and duties.

There is a long tradition of factionalism among Maltese musicians with a faction headed by a singer of high ability whose expertise is generally recognized. Such a singer does not exhibit the characteristics usually expected of a leader. He does not take any active part in initiating action, nor does he direct activities, maintain order, nor enforce decisions upon the group. Rather, he sits quietly off to one side, wearing a hat and smoking a cigar (indications of status, since no other musician wears hard-brimmed hats or smokes cigars), and is approached whenever a decision is called for. Then, and only then, does he comment quietly about a situation. His suggestions, while not overtly directive, are always followed.

Membership in a Maltese faction is continually changing. A man who is a member of one faction may, through various processes, move his relationship to the other faction, then move back to the original faction within a period of two to three years.

With the advent of commercialism in the musical situation in Malta, it was soon deemed necessary for the musicians to form a union. They did so; however, the resultant formation was not a single union, but two musicians' unions, whose membership at any given time strictly parallels membership in the factions. There is only one alteration which is made: the musicians' union has a president who is never the head of the faction. This is done because of the strong myth of egalitarianism; to flaunt one's ability by taking a public office would be inappropriate. To solve the problem, a figurehead president is elected who seeks the advice of the head of the faction before taking any action, whatsoever.

In addition to the factions and musicians' unions, "village groups" of musicians exist, as mentioned before. These musicians have nothing to do with the activities of the more formally organized men, but often center their activities around a particular bar in their home village, gathering there to perform almost every night. These are people whose musical capabilities are not sufficient to allow them to participate in the activities of the factions and unions, whose membership and activities range throughout the islands. Village groups are composed of people who cannot call on friends if asked to organize a performance.

Even within villages there may be factionalism. This is indicated spatially by the presence of two bars in which singing takes place. There are also some remnants of rivalry between neighboring villages; the people of certain villages still assert that they are bitterly opposed to the singers and guitarists of their neighbors in the next village.

It is apparent that factionalism, at least in the Maltese case, is the demonstrating principle of group organization. Since Maltese singing is direct, impromptu and occasionally insulting in nature, there is a certain amount of potential for violence, even if only verbal. It is possible that the presence of opposing factions at several levels of musical organization is indicative of the validity of the statement that factionalism tends to provide a safety valve for the expression of aggression.

Internal politics within a musicians' group is often a matter of the judicious/injudicious handling of gossip. Gossip may be a matter of self-interest -- a cultural device used by the individual to forward himself through impression-management. In a widely dispersed community, gossip may be an important method of transmitting what is happening (Paine, 1967:282). Both fiction and fact are to be included under the rubric of gossip, stressing the component of self-interest.

Another focus of emphasis is to be found in Max Gluckman's assertion that gossip acts to maintain the values of the social group (1963, 1968). He views gossip as a "hallmark of (group) membership" in which "the values of the groups are clearly asserted" (1963:313). Although gossip and scandal tend to promote unity through establishment of common membership in a group, they could also potentially destroy it except for the fact that they are regulated.

Louise Lamphere, speaking of the Navajo, claims that "through gossip, individuals not only maintain a flow of information, but control and manipulate it" (1970:6). In addition to self-promotion through impression-management, the unintended consequence of gossip among the Navajo is the definition of appropriate and inappropriate behavior:

> The details of an incident...are not as important as the interpretation of judgment which is passed on the alleged behavior of an individual. What matters is not whether an individual behaved in a particular way, but that disapproval of this type of action is communicated (loc. cit.).

Melville J. Herskovits (1937) first observed that the role of gossip is quite similar to that of witchcraft, or as Nadel (1952) would prefer, to witchcraft accusations. Herskovits contends that gossip provides informal and indirect sanctions in situations where an open, formal attack is impossible or inexpedient.

Gossip may be regarded as the interchange of information which may be true or false. The information flow which constitutes communication passes through the cultural filters of an individual, and the nature of his/her world-view affects perception both in abstract and real areas. Gossip is culturally patterned and the identification of these patterns may aid materially in understanding music.

The assumption of the existence of patterning of all

forms of human behavior with its implications of organization and process may be said to form one of the main *raisons d'etre* of ethnomusicology. If patterning does exist, and if the individual culture-bearer is the medium of information flow, gossip becomes a medium of exchange for interpretation of reality. All communication is a variety of metaphor and the distinction of what is, or is not, gossip becomes a matter of cultural awareness. As such, it provides a vital key to the identification of a particular group's most archetypal patterns.

It does not matter whether or not a piece of information is factual. The implication of a statement varies, depending upon its peculiaristic context; however, in order to understand the implications, the individual hearing or conveying the bit of gossip would have to comprehend the nature of the system and its symbols. The term "gossip" then should be restricted to the conveyance of information which requires prior understanding of the social system and the context in which it is found. Gossip in a specific society serves to identify some of its most basic values.

In Malta, the nature of gossip is predicated upon positive cultural values. Gossip is carried on primarily among the supporters of musicians rather than by the musicians, themselves. Gossip about an individual serves to support his sense of self-value. Collectively, gossip aids in the initiation, maintenance, and re-ordering of factionalism while adhering to a basic two-part model which factionalism is required to take.

Supporters of Maltese musicians move freely from wine shop to bar, to tavern, wherever singers are present. They are given admission to the performances of all groups whether they support them or not. Although they may be considered spies from the other faction, the supporters are treated with equal courtesy by all; spies are welcomed as carriers of information between factions.

The information of the Maltese supporters is not accidentally obtained, for the central figure of a faction often solicits the services of a supporter. The supporter, selected for the service of spying, maintains close contact with the leader. The relationship is informal with no pressure whatsoever placed upon the supporter to find a given performance, perhaps record it and report back to the leader. By means of the activities of several spies, the leader is kept apprised of any references to members of his group in the song duel or in conversations. It must be noted that spies are not relied upon for complete honesty and their information is often evaluated in the knowledge that supporters really would like to see a serious clash between factions.

Supporters also function in facilitating the movements from one faction to another. When it is known that a man might be considering moving from one faction to the other, he will suddenly be quoted as making fairly nice remarks about members of the opposition. The supporters, who know of his intentions although they may not have been formally stated, begin to make positive remarks about the opposing faction while down-grading their own faction of the moment. Over a period of weeks, comments become so strong that action is finally taken to invite the man to sing with the members of the other faction. Once he has done this, he is cut off from his original group and taken into the other.

In the case of Malta, gossip serves positive, practical

purposes -- allowing movement by facilitating the flow of information through indirect channels. It might be suggested at this point that gossip is often a valuable aid in understanding the workings of any society; in many cases, gossip may not be as obvious as in Malta, but the kinds of information transmitted by this route will never be purposeless.

The relationship between politics and music is by no means confined simply to musicians' groups or to the performers and their supporters. In many instances, there is a relationship between the organization of musical politics and organization of the more general political activity within the society. In Malta, there is an almost direct correspondence. The principle of bipolar opposition seems to permeate Maltese society. Boissevain (1965, 1969) reports the same kind of factionalism at the village level which is, at present, island-wide. In the area of national politics where there are actually five or six political parties, only two are regarded as important.

The dual nature of factions becomes clearer in approaching the concept of *partiti*, which Boissevain equates with factions. In the discussion of *festa partiti* on the village level, he remarks that although village unity is an ideal, all villages are divided internally by cleavages which cut across the community at various levels, some of which are only temporary, disappearing when the issues are resolved. Others have become a permanent part of the social scene and regardless of origin or duration, such divisions are acute to the villagers. He further states that "persons made vulnerable through a network of personal relations are often forced to commit themselves to a particular division. In doing so, they become opposed to neighbors and kinsmen who are committed to the other side". The Maltese call these divisions *partiti*, a term corresponding not only to "parties", but also to "factions". *Partiti* are believed to have *pika* (competition and hostility) between them (1965:74).

Musicians distinguish their factions from *partiti*, although *pika* may exist between them. Among musicians who function both at the village and national levels, at least part of the general political concept of leadership has been copied. As mentioned before, factions have leaders or heads but the president of the musicians' union is a figurehead. A similar arrangement is purported to be functioning in the Maltese government. Although the factionalism, present in the musicians' groups, exists at what might best be called a national, rather than a local level, there is some indication that factionalism reaches even to the village musicians' groups. The Maltese tendency to group things in twos (whether this is an easy feat or not) is maintained in musical life as well as in wider arenas.

It is not meant to suggest here that the political organization of musicians' groups always parallels the larger political organization of a particular society. Instead, it is suggested that this is an area for careful investigation, since insights gained at one level may be tested at other levels in order to reveal the strength of patterning of decision-making, leadership and other factors of political organization. If musical groups exhibit political organization, music itself may possibly be political as well. The exact nature of this will differ in each case in all probability. While it is logical to expect political organization within musicians' groups, not all music will be political in nature. Instead, it is reasonable to expect that some music will function in a political way.

In Malta, the long ballad form, *fatt*, sometimes serves

115

as a vehicle for political commentary. *Fatts* must refer to actual events, but some degree of commentary and interpretation is allowable. Since there is a tradition of indirection in Malta, it is not surprising that a *fatt* may progress at two levels of meaning; in one instance, a commentary on clothing fashions and their effects on the morality of the country is also interpreted as comments on the political situation. The Maltese song duel is often used as a means of discussing political dissatisfaction at various levels, although usually such remarks are in double entendre, rather than in the surface meaning.

One has only to consider the music of dissent in world perspective to find numerous examples of songs which are political in intent. The cornerstone of the Civil Rights Movement in the United States in the 1960's was "We Shall Overcome". In this case, the song states an intention, a goal and a focus of political activity.

Music is also used in some instances as a means of social control. The moralistic stories of the Malagasy *hiragasy* clearly demonstrate how one should behave, serving as a teaching device and a reminder of proper behavior and values. The *mgodo* of the Chopi (Tracey, 1948) allow for direct insults and comments upon the behavior of members of the community. In some instances, local leaders may be referred to as sneaks, thieves, or whatever might be appropriate; others are similarly chastised for breaches of custom or morality, and the entire community is reminded through public performances that they should mend their ways.

The political ramifications of not only the organization of musicians' groups, but also the various ways in which

116

political roles may be taken by musical sound, constitute an important area of study. Unfortunately, this type of investigation has not received the amount of attention and degree of focus it deserves. However, an investigation of potential political factors within music and musicians' groups coalesces a large segment of the information about music which is necessary to the understanding of the entire system.

RELIGION

The closest bond between music and any other aspect of life is with religion. In all societies, whether religion is a cultural focus or not, music plays a part in ceremonial and ritual. Because this association is so patent, the discussion of religion may be one of the richest for the study of music.

The role of music in religion is dominated by the organizational structure of particular religions. Where myth is a prominent part of public religious activities, songs are used as retention devices. Sections of a major myth cycle may be elaborated upon as the basis for highly specific stories in drama and, by this means, the memorization and retention of it is assured. Frequent public presentation allows for wider knowledge of such stories and their transmission through time.

In Tikopia where ancestor worship is the basis of the aboriginal religion, mythical creatures from the higher pantheism belong to various families. They are venerated by the recital of songs either in the context of special ceremonies celebrating the families' relationship to them, or in the general ritual presentation known as the Work of the Gods, where massive re-statements of the mythical cycle are presented in public. The Tikopian songs generally are not mythical recitations, but short, almost theatrical statements which refer to longer myths. In addition, major ancestral figures are remembered by songs (*seru*) which they, themselves, composed during their lifetimes as part of their ceremonial obligations.

The use of music in connection with the recitation of the stories of culture heroes frequently are religious in nature. In the case of Tikopia, the inclusion of culture heroes in the list of ancestors presented at the Work of the Gods is an indication of their having been raised to at least a semi-divine status.

This is also true of the Epic of Gesar of Ling as presented in Tibet, although this long story of King Gesar is rarely performed as a whole. The total presentation of the Epic would require four to six weeks, with rests for the singer. Most performers choose to sing only one chapter as their religious duty. At present, there is no way of ascertaining whether the ancient Epics were, in fact, religious in nature.

The most frequent use of music in connection with religion is as an intimate part of ceremonial and ritual. There are several possible explanations for the use of music in ritual and perhaps the most logical is also the most simple-minded. Ritual is highly patterned behavior -- and music is also highly patterned. That the two should so frequently coincide is perhaps a mark of their similarity of quality. This relationship might stem from the redundancy involved in ritual speech, music and ritual, itself.

All human action may occur in both highly structured

and unstructured forms. Music is always redundant in comparison with other forms of human activity. This is frequently expressed by stating that music is highly patterned; at other times, the repetitiveness (or redundancy) which music represents is pointed out. The distinction which can be so quickly made between music and other forms of human activity lies in the fact that music rarely, if ever, becomes unstructured. Once sound becomes unstructured, it ceases to be referred to as music.

That the patterning of music makes it a natural association for ritual, which is already patterned, is obvious; conversely, whatever is happening in music is also patterning other forms of behavior in a redundant manner. If, on the other hand, the reason for the high degree of redundancy in both ritual and music is sought, there is the possibility of investigating at least one feasible explanation. Ritual is a response to anxiety. Is music perhaps a response to anxiety, as well?

Lomax explains the redundancy of music as a group-organizing function that displays the "behavioral norms which are crucial to a culture" (1968:15). In his terms, music has two functions: to organize groups of people into activity; and to demonstrate, within that activity, certain core-concepts which represent a skeletal statement of the major values of a society. Lomax further describes music as a form of communication, in that it signals cultural patterns in specific, symbolic ways.

There are two possible explanations of the redundancy in music. First, that it is a reaction to anxiety; and second, that it is the symbolic statement, a display of the basic cultural values of a group of people. Probably the most reasonable way to examine musical redundancy is to consider the function of music in various ritual conditions. Ritual is often associated with anxiety. What role, then, does music play in ritual?

One of the most striking features of liturgical music is the length of time that forms may be retained. The primary examples must come from those societies with written, rather than oral, history. At one point in Western society, Gregorian Chant embodied all of the fixed sentiments of the Catholic mass. The credo and the other parts of the mass were sung with standard words and varying melodies. Pope Gregory (590-604) codified and arranged the liturgical chant of the Roman Catholic Church. Prior to his time, four different styles of chant had developed in the far-flung parts of Europe controlled by the Roman Church. According to ninth century writings on Gregory, he abbreviated and simplified the Sacrementary of Gelasius which represents the background for the modern Roman Missal.

Some scholars (Reverend Frederick Homes Dudden, 1926:568) doubt that all of the changes and complications in plain chant were instigated by Pope Gregory, but agree that melodic stabilization took place around his era. While the use of Gregorian Chant deteriorated markedly after the fourteenth century, it is clear that at whatever period the stabilization was created, it has lasted for at least seven centuries. Even today, the Chant is to be heard in certain circumstances.

The example of Gregorian Chant illustrates the longevity to be expected when music is associated with ritual. While in many circumstances, historical records do not clearly indicate the age of given liturgical musics, the assumption from the example of Gregorian Chant that *redundancy through time* in the sense of repetition through time, is a mark of ritualized music.

This is a frequent concept throughout the world. For a ritual to be affective, the music must be performed "correctly" or in the proper tradition. Among the Navajo, if any part of the ritual (including the music) is performed wrongly, it must be started over from the beginning. The Kutenai are not so severe as this. If a mistake occurs in the music the ceremony will not be begun again, but the performers will go back a short way to cover up the mistake.

These expressions of correctness are an indication of the way in which people view the function of music in religion. It is a set pattern, often said to have been handed down directly to men by the Gods. This has *power*; that is, if performed correctly, music reaches the ears of the supernatural.

The idea of music as the communicator with the supernatural is almost world-wide in extent and indicates a relationship which may help to understand the retentive nature of liturgical music. It is a non-human way of talking which can be understood in the spirit world. Among the Central Sakalava of Madagascar, some kinds of music are directed toward the inimicable spirits to keep them busy so that they will not harm participants during ritual moments; other music is directed at benevolent spirits who are asked to bless the proceedings.

While the question of retentiveness cannot always be checked due to the absence of historical records, there are many indications that songs are very old. In the Work of the

Gods in Tikopia, some songs use words which are now almost completely unintelligible to modern speakers of Tikopia. The explanation given for this is that the songs are extremely old and have been retained by careful repetition in their original form. While the question as to whether they are now sung as originally composed is unanswerable, the position of unintelligible song texts in the ritual is perhaps indicative: these are the songs of ancestors who died at least several centuries ago.

From these examples, it is apparent that music is regarded as a form of ritual procedure which must be performed correctly. In theory, then, historical versions of earlier musical forms should be preserved in liturgical music. Whether change has actually occurred is not possible to determine, given currently available procedures. The point is that constant and exact repetition through time is the ideal for many forms of liturgical music throughout the world. The reasons given for this are varied, but mainly relate to the idea that a particular sound pattern is in some way pleasant to the Gods.

In the Blanket Rite of the Lower Kutenai, each spirit has only one song which calls him into the ceremonial province. This particularistic relationship between a song and a supernatural being, while specific to the Kutenai, indicates that a relationship is strongly felt between music and the supernatural. The Kutenai believe that hearing their music is pleasing to the Gods. Spirits like listening to their songs as much as they enjoy smelling tobacco smoke.

Another view of the function of music can be seen in the Jazz Funeral now confined mostly to Louisiana, especially in New Orleans. One of several jazz bands may be hired to walk with the funeral procession from the church to the cemetery; large crowds usually assemble outside the church during the service. As the cortege moves out, the band plays slow, walking-hymns such as "Just A Closer Walk With Thee", as the automobiles, band and accompanying crowds move along the streets. After the short ceremony at the grave, just as the ceremonial bit of earth touches the coffin, the band turns and begins to move away, playing fast jazz. The anomalous crowd forms itself into the "second line" of dancers, strutters and actors, waving brightly colored umbrellas, bouncing babies and generally enjoying the music. Young men sometimes drop to the ground to do the "alligator" -- a dance performed by bouncing up and down on the tips of the fingers and toes.

The scene is one of total release. Those who frequently walk with the dead know this to be a moment in which the past may be wiped away through joyous music and dancing, without regard to surroundings. The heat of the sun, the rain, or the cares of the day are totally forgotten in an expiatory, cathartic form of activity. One comes away from a Jazz Funeral refreshed, renewed and somehow eased of concerns.

There are many theories as to the origin of the New Orleans Jazz Festival. The most persistent is that West Africans believe that the dead go directly to a joyous heaven upon burial. Similar scenes of joy and release are to be seen at the end of West African funerals, where the living celebrate the ascension of the dead to a state of perpetual peace and joy. The Jazz Funeral may be a retention of this idea in active form. The funeral, itself, is expiatory. It offers release of tension, a way of cleansing and purifying the mind. It revives hope, temporarily dampens worry, creating new approaches

123

to life within the few hours the event may last.

The cathartic effect of music is not well studied. As participants in many Jazz Funerals, the authors know personally, that the psychological effect of temporarily suborning one's personality to the music in a total way is a revitalizing experience. It is not trance, but it is close to trance in the sense that, for a while, the individual allows himself or herself to be swayed by the music and the scene. To the extent that one is successful in letting go, one will be more or less relieved. Listening to music and moving with it under such circumstances causes a momentary break in concentration on the pressures and problems of being alive.

One of the most common associations between music and ritual is the presence of music in what are called "rites of passage". These are those moments in human life when an individual's change of status is socially marked. Birth, puberty, marriage and death are the most frequently marked changes of status in the life of an individual.

Rites of passage frequently involve changes of states of mind for an individual. At puberty ceremonials, noise, exhaustion, starvation and exposure to fearful situations are often used to aid the initiate in changing a state of consciousness. In the midst of the fear and terror generated by the ceremony itself, initiates frequently pass into a state of mind where they no longer think of themselves in the same way as previously. During the ceremony, the individual is oftentimes described as a non-person; he or she has no status because of the passing between two statuses. Turner (1967) calls this "liminality", the state of being on the threshold. The idea is taken originally from the work of Van Gennep. Turner adds to the concepts of Van Gennep the idea that a person in a liminal state may move from mere shock to "communitas".

In communitas, the individual loses not only personality, but direct consciousness of self, moving into a temporary unity with others. This state, most usually achieved by ascetic monks, often involves a sense of complete well-being and a profound love for all mankind and all living things. While little is known about this state of mind, it is a condition so radically different from normal thinking that it has been commented upon numerous times, particularly in religious literature.

It would appear from this that exposure to extreme anxiety and shock may result in a state of consciousness which is difficult to define or explain. The fact that so many cultures in the world deliberately use fear, deprivation and exhaustion to induce communitas may mean that the results of this phenomenon is a state of mind for which all people hope. In such circumstances, music is frequently used to create a state of "other-awareness" (something similar to that of the cathartic effect of the Jazz Funeral). A description of such a ceremony may give some indication of the profound nature of the experience.

Among the Central Sakalava of Madagascar, manhood as a concept is anxiety-producing. This is so because the birth rate of the Sakalava has been markedly declining for some time, due to a decrease in fertility. The Sakalava know that they are losing population and that their very survival is threatened.

The Sakalava ceremony begins with a temporary altar called *hazomanga* (blue tree), a large pole whose end has been cut to a point, is set up. Toward evening on the first day, several groups of people begin to take on special tasks. The women of the village gather together in an enclosure and begin to sing long, commemorative songs and dance, accompanied by a two-headed drum. Songs may refer to the sacredness of the occasion, to Biblical stories, or to other subjects. The women are said not to be performing music, but simply entertaining themselves.

In the meantime, the lad to be circumcised, usually about eight years old, is carried on the shoulders of one of a group of men. They dance from place to place, presenting the child to all the houses in the village and accompany their dance by rhythmic grunting. Another group of men is elsewhere, mystically searching for the two permanent altars which will replace the temporary one, after the circumcision has taken place. These larger trees, also cut to a point at the top, represent the fully-circumcised child and his father.

Another group, headed by the musical specialists of the village, is out searching for *fanafody* (medicine) which will be applied to the forehead and body of the boy to protect him from evil spirits during the dangerous moments of the circumcision. The searchers are not singing; instead, they emit a rhythmic set of whoops and grunts which fill the night with chilling sound.

In the early morning, all the participants arrive together at the scene of the actual circumcision. Near 4:00 a.m., bulls are killed and blood is smeared on the tip of the *hazomanga* and the meat is cooked and eaten.

During the ceremony, there is a strict separation of the sexes; women gather under one tree, men under another. The oldest living male relative of the family is the leader of the ceremony and gives the feast, as "father of the sacred tree", which symbolizes family continuity through the male. His wife is the "mother"; around her head are twined the *fuli velu* (threads of life), twisted cotton strands used by the Sakalava as magical representations of the continuity and stability of life. Such threads have a protective function; they are also worn by the father and by the boy, himself, who is in the most danger.

The most important aspect of the circumcision is the way in which all participants involve themselves in music at every point. Each person has music and/or noise to accompany his or her travels throughout the night and during the playing-out of his or her position in the ceremony on the following day. Sometimes, the sounds overlap in such a way as to create almost total sound confusion.

Two basic principles arise out of this example. First, whenever noise and confusion are at a high point, some bit of ceremony takes place. The madness of the scene of the surgery, the singing, the crowding, the noise and hysteria affectively mask both circumcision and the arrival of the men with the two true *hazomanga*. This is done so as to confuse the evil spirits. Second, the most important aspects of the ceremony are performed with a high degree of casualness and by, supposedly, the wrong people. Musical specialists are to be found leading the distracting music, while women (who are not regarded as making music at all) are actually performing the most essential part of the ceremony. The *kolondoy* is for the spirits, yet it is performed by women who are only "entertaining themselves".

Aside from its supposed effect on the spirits, the effect of the use of multiple musics and noise on the boy is startling. He is exhausted, frightened and hungry. At the beginning of the morning ceremony, he is already in a state of shock. By the time the actual circumcision occurs, he is deeply unaware of his surroundings. His eyes no longer focus; his musculature is completely limp; his jaw is slack. His personality seems driven out of him and the liminality of his state is totally apparent. The Sakalava would not describe the boy as in a state of trance; this concept is reserved for other behavior.

The common association between music and noise in rites of passage has been noted previously, particularly by Needham (1972). While not nearly enough is known about the role of music in rites of passage, theory at this point can state that there is an intimate relationship of some kind between the production of overwhelming sounds (be they musical or otherwise) and the liminal state of mind.

The shock produced by this may be purposeful, although its function may not yet be established cross-culturally. The personal limbo produced by massive sound is so evident as to be one of the most easily observed characteristics in rites of passage. One of the factors in the production of this state of mind is music.

Yet another view of the function of music is widespread on the North American continent. As a general rule, American Indians regard music as a special form of communication with the supernatural which has power. While music is made by human beings, it is the vehicle for the transmission of information to and from the supernatural and the means by which situations may be changed. The function of music is essentially magical.

In the Vision Quest, a young man is given a vision by his Guardian Spirit, usually in the form of an animal which gives him power through the use of a special song. Vision Quest songs are subsequently used for whatever purpose they are best suited to. Among the Kutenai, the shaman who is to perform in the Blanket Rite where the shaman, himself, is said to dematerialize and carry messages directly to the spirits, must first have a vision of Strap before he undertakes the role. Strap is the Guardian Spirit of the piece of rawhide with which the shaman's thumbs are tied behind his back.

At the high point of the first part of the ceremony, both Strap and shaman are said to have completely dematerialized and to have taken on total spirit form. In this condition, the evanescent shaman flies through the walls of the lodge or tepee, guided to specific spirits by Strap, with whom he will return into the ceremonial precinct. The relationship between the shaman and Strap occurs through a vision of Strap which takes the form of the Strap song. Among the Kutenai, each spirit has only one song. The power of a shaman is derived directly from the singing of the Song of Strap to the spirit, who comes when called and invests the human agent with the power to become evanescent.

This is a common association among American Indians. Music communicates with and transmits power from the supernatural. It is thought of as another form of language which is directed, not toward men, but toward the Guardian Spirits believed to be in control of the universe.

In order to emphasize this, there is a frequent association between music and what has been called nonsense syllables. The texts of sacred songs among American Indians are oftentimes not in a recognizable language; instead, they appear to be isolated syllables without meaning. Herndon (1971) and Halpern (1976) have reported for the Cherokee and the Kwakiutl, respectively, that the accompanying text for religious songs or chants are a form of coded message. This accords well with the American Indian concept of a "spirit language" as opposed to human language. The full extent of the use of nonsense syllables as a coded message is as yet unknown, since the sacredness of the messages has precluded their translation to ethnographers.

As yet, the ways of speaking to the supernatural have not been fully investigated in North America. For the Cherokee, a continuum of four forms of ritual "speaking" is recognized: thinking, muttering, speaking and singing. Thinking a ritual chant is the least effective and least powerful. This form of chant is used in those cases where great force is not considered necessary to the solution of the problem. Singing a chant is regarded as the most powerful form of communication with the spirits; it is reserved for use in dire emergencies.

This concept of music as power among American Indians has led to a close association between ritual specialists and music. Those who sing are not musicians; instead, they are shamans or diviners. The function of music in this case subsumes music under religious categories so firmly that there are almost no power-free forms of music.

From a functional point of view, the relationship of music to ritual and ceremonies involving music has been seen as a device for retention; for catharsis; for the succinct expression of basic religious values; and for the creation of shock and noise in rites of passage and as a vehicle of power. In each case, there is an expression of the value of music as a carrier of something else -- a participant in holiness or sacredness. While these do not represent all of the major associations between music and ritual, they seem to be major factors. This description has omitted an account of one of the most dramatic of music's associations -- that of trance -- which is the ultimate binding of factors in religious expression.

There is no reasonable definition of trance. This human activity so removes the personality of the individual from the everyday social sphere that it is difficult to discuss its nature. Trance does not take the same form everywhere; appropriate trance behavior, although seemingly anomalous as a concept, is apparently the norm rather than the exception. Trance is at once ecstatic and culture-bound, seemingly withdrawn, yet profoundly and deeply culturally patterned. Although an extreme form of human behavior, trance is, nevertheless, human behavior. As it is the nature of our species to respond to basic patterns which are learned and transmitted from one generation to another in other areas, so it is in the case of trance.

Generally, trance might be described as a variety of atypical cultural behavior which signals a special condition. The actions which take place while an individual is in "trance" range from quiet introspection to violent, uncontrollable muscle spasms. What seemingly binds the various behaviors together is an assumption of "otherness", in which the consciousness or awareness of an individual is severely transmuted from the norm. Basically, trance is a state of mind into which a person may either slip unaware (as in the case of trance possession) or that may be induced by various means.

The close relationship between religious states and

trance states reflects an assumption of the otherness of the supernatural, which requires otherness on the part of the individual facing the supernatural. The rationale behind the assumption of this behavior is as varied as is the behavior itself. What all descriptions of trance seem to have in common is that the person is acting in ways which are beyond some norm, yet symbolically comprehensible.

Among the Central Sakalava and Vezo of Madagascar, two varieties of trance are usually found. Both involve possession by spirits. The variety of possession called *tromba* results from possession by the "Spirits of the North". The Spirits of the North is a general term for the spirits of dead kings. Nobility are considered to have special powers after death, as well as individual and special needs. They long to hear music and to assume their vaunted earthly positions. To accomplish this, they possess living persons and, through them, experience what they may not know in the ancestor world.

The Spirits of the North need not come alone. They sometimes bring other spirits with them, such as the spirits of dogs or slaves. An incident of possession occurred at the town of Belo-sur-Tsiribihina, the court of the king of the Central Sakalava, where one man was possessed by the spirit of a king and another by that of a king's dog. The latter was licking the feet of the former.

The most common association between Spirits of the North and men involves players of the case zither (*salegy*). The zither music of the West Coast consists of a rhythmic, harshly harmonic accompanying figure repeated over and over, interspersed with melodic interludes of great virtuosity.

The most important aspect of zither playing is its intimate association with the spirits of the dead. Zither players are said to be possessed by one of the Spirits of the North. Players are not taught to play by the spirits; rather, the spirits play the instruments "through" the player and afterwards the player's fingers "remember" the song. The players claim to be in trance.

Not only zither players are possessed by a Spirit of the North. Anyone who asks to hear case zither music is always willingly accommodated, since it is assumed that such interest is always instigated by a dead king.

Salegy players exhibit a serious demeanor for, to them, their introspection is a form of possession. The expression of a sober, dedicated interested player and a quiet, intent listener as two possessed people is a way of acting out the closeness which life and after-life have for the Malagasy. In the midst of a truly amazing artistic style with its trembling runs, ecstatic falls of sound and intricate musical improvisation, listener and player alike are caught in a mood of introspection in which the music is the central focus of attention. In Western terms, it is difficult to say that *salegy* players are indeed in trance; during performances, they are capable of answering questions and otherwise distracting themselves from the music.

In contradistinction to this gentle, introspective statement of awareness, the Vezo and Sakalava have another form of trance, called *bilo*, mentioned before. This term refers to a feast for the spirits; called a feast because in the more extreme cases, it is necessary to sacrifice bulls. The word, *bilo*, applies equally to the state of an individual, to the individual himself, to the rites occasioned by this state, and to the spirits present (Faublee, 1954:39). Because this is a trance possession, the spirit (*bilo*) becomes the individual when he possesses him. The *bilo* usually takes the form of dancing madness and is an extremely dangerous and incoherent form of trance possession.

The ferocity of behavior in persons possessed by *bilo* is said to be exorcised only by "dancing them out". The spirits must be made to go away by the process of regularizing the motions of a possessed person. Musicians are absolutely necessary for this purpose, since the presence of rhythmic music reduces the arbitrariness and incoherence of the body movements of possessed people. As the sound of music penetrates the mind of the possessed, he or she begins to regularize motions of feet and hand until they are actually dancing. When the individual drops to the ground exhausted, the *bilo* has been chased away.

In this exaggerated form of trance, one sees a relationship to the activities of the circumcision ceremony where the *kolondoy* is also played. Just as this form is used to drive spirits out of the possessed person in the *bilo*, in the circumcision ceremony, it is used to prevent possession of the initiate by evil spirits.

These two examples of trance within the same society, different as they are from one another, indicate the range of behavior which may be involved in the concept. In the case of the Sakalava, the diversity of behavior is supported by a belief that there are benevolent and inimicable spirits. Thus, two different approaches to the supernatural result from an assumed difference between types of spirits. From these examples, it is possible to determine the cultural patterning involved in the concept of trance.

It is interesting to note that in Madagascar, dancing madness is a response to upsetting situations. Epidemics of dancing madness in which entire villages or towns have been seized with the impulse to dance have been mentioned in the literature. In each case, the individuals have been upset by political or religious decisions on the part of their rulers. One can speculate, therefore, that dancing madness serves two purposes, only one of which may be religious. As an attention-getting device for an individual who is troubled, dancing madness is unparalleled.

Dancing madness is an exceedingly dangerous state. If the *bilo* cannot be driven out of the body of a person through the exhaustion of dancing, that person may die, for the general musculature of the body seems to lock, resulting in uncontrollable behavior. Among the Betsileo of the Central Plateau, an episode of dancing madness which is not quickly cured is regarded as a sign of supernatural power. If the spirits will not leave an individual's body, the individual becomes theirs. At the same time that the *bilo* is a mark of social anxiety or personal upset, it is also an indication of the possibility that a person may be the vehicle for communication with the other world.

The concept of trance as a vehicle for communication with the other world is common in West Africa and in Afro-American communities. In West Africa, most cultures do not have a centralized religion. Instead, each god has its own cult. Individuals are "called" to become members of one cult or another by special circumstances which indicate the god which has chosen him or her. For example, Shango is the god of lightning. Those who are struck by lightning and survive know that they have been called to his cult. Cult worship in West Africa involves possession of cult members by the god or gods involved during established rituals. Percussion orchestras play the music of the god, and he or she "comes to the head" of various members of the order. The god is believed to physically enter the body of the worshippers through the head during such ceremonies; the people in trance then dance out the desires of the god.

This form of trance possession is not as chaotic and uncontrolled as that of *bilo*. Each cult contains some people who do not go into trance and who are designated as helpers of those who do. Those who go into trance generally act out certain characteristics of the cult god through body motions. Trance is controlled by the ritual setting in which it occurs and ends when the ceremony ends. This more controlled form of trance, the commonest form throughout the world, still involves both music and dancing.

The shamans of the Kutenai Blanket Rite are also considered to be in trance. The songs of the Blanket Rite Ceremony are in three sections. In the first section, attention is focused on songs which will cause the shaman to dematerialize. In the second section, his dematerialized spirit, guided by Strap, is said to be seeking out spirits to bring into the ceremonial precinct to answer questions and aid members of the community. In the third section, songs are directed toward spirits who help the shaman to dematerialize. At the end of the ceremony, he has been returned to human form.

Informants described the shaman's condition as similar to that of hypnosis. He is taken over, guided and controlled absolutely by the spirit world. His body melts before him. First his thumbs dematerialize and the strap falls through them. Second, he becomes light and begins to float off the ground. Third, he comes in two in the middle and the ropes

136

tied around his waist fall away. Finally, he disappears altogether. In the process, the shaman himself undergoes the metaphysical shift from human to non-human. He is a will-o-the-wisp with no mind of his own. His whole being is put at the service of his community and of the spirit world and he rides upon the wind, guided by Strap, to seek out the forces of the Universe.

Is this trance? It is so described by the Kutenai; yet it differs markedly from the other examples given here. The shaman induces trance in himself. He places himself at the service of the supernatural, rather than the other way around. His function as a ritual specialist is an important one in the community and the position of shaman is both feared and revered. Like all shamans in the Circumpolar cultures, he is regarded as different from other men, in that his special powers remove him from normal human life in many ways. In those cultures exhibiting shamanism, people who do not fit well within the social fabric frequently become shamans through the acceptance of their difference from others.

Whatever specific forms it may take, it is clear that the relationship between music and ritual is extremely close. This provides an intensely fertile ground for ethnographic investigation, one which has long been utilized productively.

CONCLUSION

The relationship between music and culture, which has often been asserted, is indeed present. What scholars have mainly referred to in these statements is the close association of music with economics, politics and religion. This association can be viewed in three ways: (1) that cultural institutions limit musical expression; (2) that certain cultural institutions provide organizational models for musical groups; (3) that music functions within culture as a means of shifting personal awareness.

5

COGNITION AND VALUE JUDGMENTS

This chapter deals with the general mental processes and decisions made about musical systems and music concerning cognition and value judgments. This is the area of categorization about the musical context which is sometimes highly specific and sometimes diffuse.

COGNITION

Cognition is a term which is used in its most general sense for all modes of being conscious or aware of an object, whether that object is material or intellectual. It is an ultimate mode of consciousness: strictly the presentation of an item of consciousness, whether through sensation or otherwise. It also involves judgment; the distinction of one object or idea from others.

Generally speaking, the concept of cognition takes for granted that there is a distinction between the mind that knows and the object or idea which is known. It takes no account of the metaphysical and ontological problem concerning the possibility of a relation between the ego and the non-ego, but assumes that such a relation does exist. Cognition, then, is a term used to refer to *modes of awareness and perception*. It includes rules, maps, strategies and routes of perception.

In order to understand the nature of perception, it is first necessary to know what knowledge is; but in order to know the nature of knowledge, one must first recognize that all knowledge is cultural knowledge. To understand cultural knowledge, one must first have an awareness of the nature of culture which is tighter than that previously presented in this text.

The concept of culture, while central to the study of anthropology, is not defined in a unitary manner. It is a much cherished concept, but one which is often misunderstood or loosely used. There is no "true" meaning of the term; instead, culture has a large number of overlapping and occasionally contradictory meanings. Perhaps the most general and most widely used meaning of the term is the omnibus definition of culture -- culture is the ways of man. Such a definition includes the thoughts, behaviors, beliefs, institutions and artifacts of human beings. While this definition is useful as a rationale for many diverse studies, it is not particularly helpful in the present consideration.

Two definitions of culture which may be of use in a consideration of cognition and value judgments are more behavioral and specific in nature. Harris has remarked that:

> ...the culture concept comes down
> to the behavior patterns associat-
> ed with particular groups of peo-

ple, that is to "customs" or to a people's way of life (1951:16).

A second definition, more clearly related to cognition, excludes behavior and restricts the concept of culture to mental constructs such as ideas, beliefs and knowledge. Such a consideration of culture has emerged primarily from linguistics.

Ward Goodenough suggests that "A society's culture consists of whatever it is one has to know or believe in, in order to operate in a manner acceptable to its members and to do so in any role they accept for themselves". He says that culture is not a material phenomenon consisting of things, people, behavior, or emotions; but rather, an organization of these things. "It is the forms of things that people have in mind, their models for perceiving, relating, and otherwise interpreting them" (1957:167).

Although there has been some movement toward a total divorce between behavior and mental constructs, the question involved is merely one of emphasis. Following the practice of Werner and Fenton (1971), the authors will speak of cultural behavior and cultural knowledge, or behavior and knowledge, implying that both are cultural. For this purpose, the concern is with the nature of cultural knowledge as well as its potential shaping of cultural behavior.

Cultural knowledge is not to be equated with an ultimate reality, nor should it be taken for granted that reality is perceived similarly by all people. Some items of knowledge may appear to be perfectly obvious. The sounds made by a bird, the odor of gasoline, the brightness of a star may all be perceived, for such events are encountered directly by the

141

senses. However, even at the empirical level of knowledge, all people do not perceive things in the same way or with the same degree of intensity. Nor does the same individual always perceive the same stimulus in a consistently identical manner. In the non-empirical realms of the mind, knowledge becomes even more diffuse and difficult to discuss, investigate or explain.

Cross-cultural studies have shown that the way people conceive of their environment and the universe differs radically from one society to another, and that what people take for reality is socially constructed (Berger and Luckmann, 1966). Within a given culture, information is categorized in patterned ways. These patterns are part of the arbitrary universe of human cultural behavior. They result from percepts and the formulation of concepts within a cultural setting and it is in this manner that human beings are able to communicate with one another, creating conceptual roles which are vastly removed from sensory experiences.

Knowledge is received, stored and processed by the mind. What is known is not simply a copy of material objects and signs in our environment. Information is channeled through a physical receptor and converted in the human neurological system to a percept. For example, if a man is playing a flute, this may have various meanings to those who hear him; but before they can make use of those meanings, they must first perceive that "sound" is happening. The percept of this event is not the flute, the man, or the music. When the vibrations of air reach the ear, the information changes form so that it may be transmitted to the brain where it is then stored as a percept. Other sensory stimuli are transformed and stored in a similar way.

The universe of incoming information confronts an individual with an infinitely varying, complex set of percepts. Without some means of sorting information, a person would soon be lost in the uniqueness of each event, object or perception. The chaos of incoming information is reduced to manageable form through the formulation of concepts.

In this process, human knowledge is transformed from a large number of percepts to a limited and manageable number of concepts. Human beings learn to give attention to some features or events and to ignore others; but in most cases, concepts arise out of several sensory inputs. At this point, some of the "sounds" of flute-playing are ignored and others emphasized.

In order to cope successfully with the flood of incoming sensory stimuli, one must have some means of sorting and classifying them. The categories of concepts and the interrelationship of concepts which result are arbitrary and are generally agreed upon by most of the members of an individual's group. The final concept of "flute-playing" is the result of such categories.

The study of cognition is concerned with cultural knowledge as it has been received, transformed into percepts, sorted into concepts and sets of concepts and communicated to others. Musical cognition is the portion of knowledge which deals not only with the learning of music, but also how that learning is structured; how an individual conceives of and classifies various points of focus within music; how groups evaluate performance, instruments, styles, events and all other points of focus within that which they designate as music.

The idea of cognition is not a new one. It has been a

topic of interest to scholars in many disciplines: anthropology, economics, linguistics, psychology and sociology. It should also be mentioned that during the sixties and seventies, a number of anthropologists tried to achieve more rigor in their ethnographic method. Their work has been referred to as the new ethnography or ethnoscience (Sturtevant, 1964), or as ethnographic semantics or ethnosemantics (Kay, 1970).

Whatever terms are chosen, the study of the nature of cultural knowledge about music will provide us with a key to deepening the understanding of the nature of this phenomenon. Music is an arbitrary structuring of sound into pattern. Since this pattern is culturally conceived, culturally produced, culturally perceived, it is clear that an understanding of the mental process and categories of any given group may lead, ultimately, to the establishment of a basis for understanding the central question of ethnomusicology: What is the nature of music?

KINDS OF COGNITION

It has been repeatedly asserted that music alters awareness; some scholars speak of music as heightening the awareness. As with discussion of altered states of consciousness, however, it is meaningless to assert that something is altered or heightened without knowing what an unaltered or unheightened state might be. A search for a pragmatic approach to ascertaining the kinds of effects, generally speaking, of music on the perceiver as well as the performer of music leads to a meager inventory of clues at this point of time. Much work will have to be undertaken before it can be said with any degree of certainty what music does to human perception.

Not unexpectedly, it was Charles Seeger who pointed out a basic distinction within the musical experience. He has suggested that one should distinguish between two modes of discourse -- speech, or *talking* about music; and music, or *making* music:

> The relationship of the (intrinsic) music-rationale known by the musician to any of the (extrinsic) speech-rationales of music or to the whole collection of them constitutes one of the fundamental problems of musicology (Seeger, 1960:225).

This is an opposition which Herndon (1974:244) termed "Seeger's dilemma". Although Seeger was not referring directly to kinds of cognition, he was pointing to the differences in cultural knowledge between the performing of music and the knowing *about* music. Similarly, a distinction might be made at a very basic level between performing music and *hearing* music, with a third distinction between either hearing or performing music and simply talking *about* it.

These are basic, broad, and -- as yet -- unproved distinctions or categories; nevertheless, they are useful assumptions within musical systems. In a particularistic sense, there are several areas which may now be investigated by the scholar; these include rules, maps, strategies, routes and events.

RULES

Human knowledge, as stated earlier, is shaped by what

is selected and how that selection of experience is transformed by the learning process. The sensory input is never everything which can be perceived or even an objective sampling of it because one selects the stimuli which will reach the brain. This may be especially true of visual and auditory stimuli. At a concert, one is not usually aware of the sound of the air conditioning or heating system, paying little attention to coughs, rattling of programs, squeaking of seat backs or scuffling of feet unless these become fairly intense. Thus, knowledge is selective and awareness is, in many cases, culturally determined.

There are rules governing the selection of important or marked behavior and cognition. For cognition, rules may be stated in varying degrees of specificity. This specificity does not imply that rules should be equated with laws, however. In the realm of the mind, things become extremely arbitrary.

Although there are potentially thousands of combinations of ways to identify, use and classify aspects of experience, they will not all be used in any one culture. Cultural behavior is customary behavior -- which means that human thought and action does not occur randomly, but is put together in a patterned manner. Each society selects only a small portion of the actions and thoughts which are humanly possible. For example, each language involves the selection of fewer than 60 of the indefinite number of vocal sounds which human beings are capable of producing. In a similar manner, each human group utilizes only a restricted number of pitches, selected out of the universe of pitch variation through the traditions of the group in question.

There are conditions which restrict not only the range but also the patterning of human behavior. One kind of restriction involves the rules which are learned by members of a society. This is certainly not the only kind of restriction on behavior but it is an important area of consideration.

It is fairly clear that a distinction should be made between the "real" and the "ideal". That is, some rules refer only to ideal behavior while others refer to actual behavior taking place. This can create severe difficulties. Some ideal rules are only statements of historical practice and have very little to do with current action.

It is said, for instance, that a Cherokee ceremony requires four different kinds of singing specialists. While this may have been true in the past, it is no longer the practice. This would have to be interpreted as a historic ideal, rather than a reflection of ritual practice at the present time. It is necessary to distinguish carefully between those statements which are ideals never realized, or not currently realized, and those statements and rules which are actually followed.

Another area of possible confusion arises in the distinction to be made between rules and concepts which an individual can formulate with clarity and those rules which are only vaguely stated. It is probable that a specialist may be able to formulate rules which the majority of a population would never consider. Therefore, it is probably necessary to delineate a level of expertise before rules are discussed.

It is also necessary to remember that rules, as aspects of human knowledge, have their locus in the mind. Like a program stored in a computer, human rules are made up of bits of information stored in the brain which are used to process other information as well as to organize and direct behavior. Like a number of other mental phenomena, rules

147

can be represented by symbols outside the mind. While rules are known by an individual, that individual may not be able to state them explicitly or clearly; nor will a person necessarily be able to replicate the totality of rules stated by any one else. Like the grammar of the language, many rules are difficult to verbalize, although they may be understood in practice and tacit in knowledge.

Each person actually knows more than he/she can relate, verbally. Recognizing a person's walk, stance, head movements, features of face of uniqueness of voice is a matter of intuitive recall -- one that is extremely difficult, if not impossible -- to describe in words. This type of knowledge, such as rules of human behavior within a culture, is known and understood, but often simply cannot be placed within the limitations of vocabulary.

Certainly, not all kinds of human knowledge about music are impossible to verbalize; in fact, one might find one's informants verbalizing more than one can deal with. However, it remains a task for the researcher to formulate the tacit rules which members of a group are using in order to create their music, as well as those rules which are stated by members of a given society.

It should be remembered that rules are learned at different levels, also. This, in turn, determines the effect of those rules on behavior. In Malta, it was discovered that there were several singers who were unaware that a good singer rarely mentions the central subject of the song duel directly more than once in a song, in most contexts. These singers would simply repeat the subject of the duel continually, providing a source of amusement for those singers who did understand the rules, and who encouraged the unaware singers to continue their incorrect practice.

There is probably an infinite number of gradations of learning involved in the internalization of a musical system. A child who says "me done it" has not quite learned some grammatical rules; similarly, when a child is learning to play an instrument, mistakes will be made. The levels of learning begin with an individual who has just heard about a new rule. It may not be understood or even recognized as a rule if it is not presented as such. At the other end of the spectrum is the person who has learned the rules so well and internalized them so thoroughly, that he or she may not be able to speak of them except in the most metaphorical terms.

In Malta, a master singer stated that "the *bormliza* is the stringing together of pearls" and was fully satisfied that he had clearly stated the boundaries of that particular musical form. It was only when the lesser singers began to talk about this form that more explicit rules were stated; that it involved singing soprano and "moving the voice around a lot".

While there are probably an infinite number of degrees to which a rule or a set of rules can be learned, it may be of help to consider the five levels proposed by Spiro in connection with learning the concepts of an ideology:

> (a) The actors have *learned about* the ideological concept, i.e., they have been exposed to it in some manner, ranging from formal instruction to informal gossip.
>
> (b) The actors have not only learned about the concept, but

they also *understand* the meaning that a text or a key informant attributes to it.

(c) Understanding its meaning, the actors believe the concept to be right or true or valid.

(d) Constituting a salient element in their cognitive systems, the concept serves to inform the actors' *behavioral* environment (as Hallowell calls it) and to structure their world.

(e) In addition to its cognitive salience, the concept has been internalized as an important element in the actors' motivational system, so that it serves not only to guide, but also to instigate, behavior (1966:1163).

It becomes clear that the researcher must make every effort to determine an approximate level to which concepts or rules have been apprehended by informants.

Perhaps one of the best means for arriving at an understanding of the rules of cognition is to be found in their negative applications. For example, marriage is a rather amorphous concept in most of its definitions and it is only by a careful examination of the way in which divorce and property settlements are handled that some of the basic aspects of marriage in a given society can be discovered.

Generally, if a society customarily requires that the former husband return his wife's dowry upon divorce, it may be assumed that the dowry has an important symbolism in marriage.

For musical investigations, two approaches are possible in the use of negative aspects to discover the meaning of the rules. First, one may investigate the manner in which rules are broken by individuals who are still learning a style or who are not achieving an extremely high level of competence in it. Second, one may investigate the manner in which rules are bent and finally broken by those people whose innovative powers cause them to exceed the bounds of prescribed custom and to create new forms and, thus, create new rules of musical behavior.

In Malta, the authors were privileged to witness the formation of a new approach to guitar playing. Maltese guitar playing has changed over the past 60 years, but basically requires the musician to improvise. Each key contains certain traditional melodic "bits" which are combined differently each time the guitarist plays in that particular key. Innovation occurs in minute detail for the most part. In the eyes of the guitarist, a new composition does not need to be a totally new piece; all that is required is a new interplay of existing material. At the beginning of this century, the guitar was almost entirely chordal. Recently, true melodies appear as the result of past innovations of several fine guitarists, and the present forms involve an interplay of melody types against one another.

In the beginning career of the average Maltese guitarist, innovation takes the form of instantaneous, impromptu re-ordering of a limited repertoire of melody-types. Most soloists have a stock of 20 to 30 melody-types which may occur in any order or at any range. Within the space of three or four phrases, a guitarist may use only one or as many as six melody types. The final phrase, or *tegbla* (fall), is more stable. About 10 to 12 patterns of falling 16th and 32nd notes are used as cadential patterns, with each pattern one phrase in length. This places the guitarist's innovation within the same category as the improvisation of early 20th century New Orleans Jazz players, where the instrumental "breaks" usually involved such a re-ordering of basic material, plus a cadential pattern. The step from germinal idea to final song takes place at once without the intervention of time for consideration or the working out of new patterns.

In spite of the fact that the Maltese state an ideal need for constant creativity in which a performer never repeats himself within an entire lifetime of playing, forms must remain stable in order to allow for the type of innovation Maltese playing requires. In such a situation, stability of form is a prerequisite to performance and one should not expect new forms to arise easily.

However, a new form has arisen. It is called *kitteri bis* (guitars only). It may be the invention of one man, Indri Brincat, a guitarist who is undoubtedly the best of the Maltese performers. In *kitteri bis*, there are no singers and any style of music can be played. The only means of identification is by the name of the key. Changes are occurring which may eventually lead Brincat completely out of the realm of Maltese folk music as it is now known. As *kitteri bis* is presently played, two layers of development may be seen. At first, Mr. Brincat was imitating the local style faithfully. The guitar soloist merely "sang" the singers' parts and then supplied an intervening interlude. In time, Brincat began to elaborate his playing; several singer melodies could be heard in a given guitar performance, making Brincat's playing a catalog of recent musical history in Malta.

In the intervening interlude, the four-phrase structure so carefully presented by most guitarists began to disappear. It was replaced by phrase structures of any length, up to and including the total interlude. Melody types, as a concept, were still present in Mr. Brincat's playing but they were rapidly merging into other, more complex statements involving diminution, inversion, recapitulation and other variation forms.

During the second layer of development, the statement of the singer's melody came to have less importance. The strophe became less clear, melodic content became almost skeletal and traditional chord lines began to be questioned. Mr. Brincat began teaching his accompanying guitarist new chordal combinations, all of which were practiced with ferocity. Shifts from major to minor occurred within a single performance, triple meters appeared and exaggerated accelerandos developed. Thus, one man had so thoroughly broken with tradition as to create a totally new form. He developed it out of traditional material, slowly shifting his emphasis until improvisation broke the bonds that held the form stable.

This did not occur without repercussions, for Malta is not a society which allows change to override tradition easily. The composer, the creator, the innovator in any sphere of customary action is literally taking his chances. Mr. Brincat, recognized as the greatest of the living Maltese guitarists, was chastised indirectly and later ostracized because the other musicians felt that he was no longer playing traditional Maltese material. In their criticisms of his playing, the other musicians revealed quite clearly the boundaries of traditional Maltese folk music. By following the ideal statement rather than the practice, Brincat had broken another set of rules and, in changing the musical form, had encountered a high degree of resistance.

This example indicates that, although they may not be verbalized directly, there will be rules for performance in all styles. These may be stated clearly or indistinctly, but they will be known to the performers, however. It is vital for the scholar to attempt to discover, through whatever means may be available, as many levels and forms of rules as possible.

There are at least two caveats to the study of rules for musical behavior, as there are for any kind of cognitive study. It has been mentioned that there is a distinction to be made between real and ideal behavior. In many ways, this dichotomy represents an over-simplification. There is usually an ideal pattern in most cultures -- that behavior which the society members feel is appropriate or "proper" and/or "normal" -- and that behavior which is the real behavior or what members of the society actually *do*. There is also that behavior which is presumed or assumed which is action(s) that members of a group *assume* its members perform.

Clearly, there is no guarantee that the rules inferred by an observer of behavior are the same as the rules employed by the person or persons performing the observed activity. Nor can whatever devices an observer may construct in order to account for behavior ever be a full representation of the mental phenomenon which generated the behavior.

That is, cognitive descriptions and models do not replicate on paper the actual perceptual processes of the people studied. Cognitive explication of rules is a means of explanation of behavior which, while it may approach an actual process or reasoning, does not and should not claim to replicate it.

MAPS

One aspect of human sensory input rarely investigated is that dealing with human mapping procedures. This is the area dealing with the concepts formed by humans regarding where in space events are found, as well as those mental domains which might be called semantic space.

Consider the following English words: city, county, state, courtyard, neighborhood, exit. This list includes several different kinds of space. Everyone has a set of spatial categories, only some of which are shared. Events take place in space; objects occupy it, are separated by it and move through it. There has been much attention in various disciplines paid to physical space, but little scholarly notice has been taken of the symbolic and expressive aspects of space. These subjective aspects are less easily measurable than physical space and it may be that such investigation, of necessity, has had to await the discovery and development of cognitive methodologies.

In investigating the symbolic and expressive aspects of space, one might include the ways people experience space, how they make use of it, and how they are influenced by it. Some space (such as the internal structuring of buildings, cities or towns) is fixed in nature and not readily changeable. Other aspects of space such as furniture, screens, curtains, or other items are movable. At the smallest level there is what might be called individual space or microspace, which includes human use of the space surrounding one.

In the consideration of cognition, the discussion of mapping will be limited to what is generally called "social space". That is, the concern with the question: "Where are you?" Social space is multi-dimensional.

In order to describe an individual or a group location, choices must be made as to frame of reference. For example, the question, "Where is the Micmac Indian Reservation?" might be answered in a number of ways: (1) 48 degrees North, 67 degrees West, in North America, the province of Quebec, Bonaventure County; (2) about 350 miles north of Boston; (3) up North; (4) down South. Each description would be appropriate in some context. In each case, however, there are culturally derived categories which indicate and delimit spatial dimensions.

Areas of social space are generally associated with particular social groups in most instances. The territory of a tribe or nation is given a geographic locus. Thus, one can speak of the Tikopia occupying a certain island as opposed to those islands occupied by the Maltese. Or one can speak about the Eastern Band of Cherokee who live in North Carolina as opposed to the Western Cherokee who live in Oklahoma. Within a generalistic geographical territory, there are boundaries which may be a matter of dispute, but are always forms of cultural conventions. The links between groups and their territory are likely to be quite strong.

One has only to consider the historical removal of Indian tribes from the East to the area west of the Mississippi River in order to begin to understand this concept. Territories are often defended, especially those which have some form of "no trespassing" sign on them. Boundaries are thus strongly linked to human groups.

Access to certain areas of social space are often used to mark status. This marking may be used to distinguish between high and low status as well as sacred and profane status. For example, in New Guinea, boys may not enter the men's house until initiated and women may never enter it. Similarly, in Madagascar, the noble's head has to be higher than anyone else's for various ceremonial and religious reasons.

In matters of protocol and rank, space is used in motion to play out status; most obviously demonstrated by processions and banquets. In some societies, one's place in a procession is a clear mark of rank in that society; the highest rank is sometimes last; sometimes first. At banquets, there may be a clear illustration of rank based on where one sits. These boundaries are arbitrary in nature because what indicates high status territorially in one society may indicate low status in the next. It is the general use of concrete spatial relations in the statement of relative status which is the justification for the more abstract notion of social space.

People live where they do in part because they "know their place". There is generally some equivalent in almost every society of the American notion of "living on the right or wrong side of the tracks". In some instances, musicians are placed high up in the ranks within a society and their dwelling places in a town or village indicate this; in other instances where musicians are not well regarded, they may be placed literally on the other side of the garbage dump.

All of this kind of space discussion may be thought of

as "horizontal space", as opposed to the "vertical space" of class distinction and the personal space of kinesics.

Social space is recognized in the individual and can be investigated cognitively through the formulation of cognitive maps. A cognitive map is a spatial representation of the mental concept of locus. For music, this is of several orders. It may include not only where music is found, but also such things as the locus of an individual musician within the hierarchy of musicians of a particular kind or the restrictions on musical performance by the environment.

One important kind of cognitive map which may be collected is that of musical forms. It should be obvious that a person adept at a particular genre of music, while he/she may be cognizant of the others, will be partial to his/her own kind. The answer to the question, "What kinds of music are there in X?" will be weighted, depending upon the perspective of the person being asked the question. By collecting a number of these maps of musical forms, some idea can be attained as to a more generalized ranking of importance of various forms and styles.

A similar mapping can be obtained of musical instruments. It was only through persistent inquiry as to the kinds of instruments available in Malta that knowledge was gained of the stone whistle (which is now used by children, generally) and of the one man on the islands who is still capable of making Maltese bagpipes.

It is possible that some instruments not in general use may be discovered through the process of collecting a number of mental maps of musical instruments. It is likely that much information will be gathered regarding the nature of instruments, the ranking of their importance to each individual and, perhaps by extension, such information as fictive statements regarding the place of each instrument in the general hierarchy of sound.

Perhaps the most important and productive of the mental maps to investigate are those regarding the occasion. As an illustration, a brief sketch will be given of the main musical occasions in Malta.

THE *XALATA*

There is a strong tradition in Malta of singing folk songs while riding in a cart, a type of activity called the *xalata*. Private hire buses have replaced the frequency of carts, but prior to World War II, at least two singers and one guitarist would spend the entire night riding around the island in a cart, singing and playing. Many romanticized stories are told of the cart and donkey plodding through the narrow streets of a rival village, its occupants well fortified with wine, singing the praises of their own village and denigrating the rival.

Today, the *xalata* is confined almost exclusively to warm, summer weekends when groups of people hire a bus for this purpose. Such groups fall into three categories: (1) families, mostly women and children with an occasional man; (2) prostitutes; and (3) men. Each *xalata* participant pays a small fee to secure a place on the bus; large baskets overflowing with wine, beer, melon, rabbit, chicken, bread and fruit are prepared. On the appointed afternoon, the merrymakers gather and pack into the bus.

When the *xalata* is a family gathering, there is a pre-

159

dominance of older women and children, with perhaps a man to lead the singing and provide rudimentary guitar accompaniment. Everyone sings, including the bus driver, who often pays more attention to the singing than his driving.

When the *xalata* is composed primarily of men and small children, the agenda is much the same. The men do not sing isolated verses or those made famous by others as the women do, however, but prefer to compose their own, creating dialogues with other singers. No attempt is made, here, to organize a formal song duel, but any number of singers can and do carry on informal discussion in song.

The outings organized by prostitutes are much the same as those of men and family groups, according to all available information. Secondary sources had to be used and, according to some of the young unmarried male singers reportedly invited to join these trips, the prostitutes are fully capable of constructing their own verses in the proper style, as the men do. The subject matter of their songs is rather bawdy for the most part.

In addition to the weekend *xalata*, it is traditional for villagers to celebrate on the day following the feast of their village patron saint. Since the feast day is usually on a Sunday, these events are usually held on Monday. The people form a line of cars, trucks, motorcycles and buses, having decorated their vehicles beforehand with paper streamers, palm branches, religious pictures or printed signs. Singing, eating and merrymaking is much the same as on any other *xalata*; however, a special verse or verses is written each year especially for the occasion. These special verses may be written by anyone and are quickly passed along to the entire group; but they must be different from those of previous years.

THE *PROGRAMM*

The musical occasion which involves taping or live broadcast of a program for the Maltese Rediffusion, or television, is distinguished by the term, *programm*. The *programm* is a specific length, usually much shorter than the normal time span of a song and is taped for later broadcast, since officials have learned that they must censor the singers. The *programm* is a paid performance, with a six-month or one-year contract between the Musicians Unions and Maltese Rediffusion; the television *programm* is made under specific contract with the individual and is for one to six broadcasts. The radio *programm* is recorded by members of one Union on Saturday evening and by members of the other Union on Thursday.

The *programm* on Maltese television is usually done in connection with a folklore series. In such cases, the music involved is minimal. One to four singers and three guitarists will be asked to play and sing for perhaps five minutes to illustrate the comments of a local folklorist; the songs taking various forms, depending upon the perceptive abilities of the folklorist conducting the *programm*.

THE *SERATA*

The *serata* is any paid performance which is not for broadcast purposes and is, with the exception of informal non-paid music, the most common musical occasion. A *serata* may be held anywhere, but must be in a public place with an audience and with paid performers. Bars, football clubs, band clubs, cinemas, hotels, restaurants, political rallies or private parties are the most usual locations. Payment may either be prearranged with a sum for each performer, a large meal at the end of the evening, or both.

The singing is more careful and more rigidly structured at a *serata* than when singers gather casually. Timing is less precise than for a *programm*; however, if there are tape recorders present, every effort will be made to have the end of a song duel coincide with the end of a tape. The *serata* usually lasts for a defined length of time which is agreed upon beforehand. At a *serata*, music will continue for slightly more than an hour per song; afterwards, the singers and guitarists pause for refreshment, resuming their activity after ten minutes or so. A song duel will usually be the first offering and during the course of the evening, there will be a predominance of this style. This may be followed by a *fatt*, or a *kitteri bis* section, or a *bormliza*.

The audience is usually quiet during the singing, particularly if a tape recording is being made. They drink and smoke but confine conversation to whispered exchanges; gossip erupts in the breaks between pieces.

THE *FESTA*

Certain feast days, or *festas*, are considered to be feasts of singing. These include the feasts of Victoria at Melliha in the first part of September; Santa Marija at Gozo in late August; San Gregor at Marsaxalokk on the first Wednesday after Easter; Lapsi (Ascension) at Xghajra; and Imnarja (the feast of St. Peter and St. Paul) at Boskett in the end of June. All the feast days (with the exception of the Imnarja) are much the same. Musicians gather, people appear in large numbers, picnic lunches are brought and singing is relatively informal.

Where there are musicians, the crowd is silent and attentive and it is on these occasions that the *fatt* singer is at his best. He may sing for forty-five minutes to an hour of a gory murder while everyone listens intently, with some audience members mouthing every word of this extremely long song. When the *fatt* ends, no one applauds or thanks the singer; it is as if he did not exist and he quietly disappears into the crowd. There is also the singing of song duels, which may be accompanied by the aggressive tape recording of the duels by supporters.

The Imnarja, in reality, marks a different kind of occasion which includes two separate activities at the same time. The main portion of this *festa* is centered in Buskett Gardens where there are produce and livestock exhibits with prizes and a competition for singers. The general activity of this feast spans a three-day period rather than the usual one-day event for villages.

At the singing competition (which is arranged by folklorists), the rules are quite different from the usual competition. Wooden platforms are erected and spotlights set up. Three or four judges, prominent professional people from the city who know nothing about the musical style, sit behind the musicians seemingly paying no attention to them. Musicians must register for the competition. A singer is hired by the folklorist to reply to the contestants as a foil in the song duel competition. Subjects are assigned usually by picking them out of a hat, and it is expected by the judges that the subject of the song duel will be repeated in every verse. At other occasions, this would be regarded as a serious breach of the rules.

Although it was once the highlight of the *festa*, the singing competition is now entered only by mediocre singers and guitarists. This is due to the rumor that the judges can be bribed as well as the fact that the judges know nothing of the intricacies of folk music.

Elsewhere on the grounds, a song competition will take place lasting from early afternoon through to the following morning. Songs on these occasions are extremely long, with song duels running more to the level of endurance contests than on other occasions.

THE *COMPETITION*

The *competition* is an event in which a private individual, usually a bar owner, offers a silver cup or other trophy as prize. The individual secures the services of one or more respected singers as judges and asks two to four contestants to pit their wits against one another until one of them makes a mistake and is eliminated. The actual form taken by song duels in a *competition* may vary; rules are set up for each event. The audience includes only musicians and avid supporters, mostly by invitation.

Everyone present considers himself a judge and lively arguments ensue as to which singer is the best. Nor is the decision of the judges considered to be final. Each person has his own opinion, which he will transmit to the general public at the outcome of the *competition*, whether or not the cup is awarded to his favorite.

THE *SFIDA*

The *sfida*, or challenge, is also between two singers or two guitarists. Although it resembles the *competition*, it is initiated by the musicians themselves rather than by a bar owner or other individual seeking publicity. The *sfida* is a challenge of not only the singer's musical ability, but also of his entire personality. There are often rumors of a *sfida*, but few actually occur. In these, there is no judge for it is merely a match of destruction in which no one can emerge as a victor.

CHRISTMAS EVE

On Christmas Eve, it is traditional for musicians to gather in the village of Zejtun in one of two bars. Despite the fact that it is customary for Maltese families to spend this evening together at home and then attend Midnight Mass, these men leave their homes to spend the night in music and drinking. Singing is informal, the bar is crowded but relatively quiet, and people spill out of it into the narrow alleyway in front. As many as eight to ten men are involved in the song duel, but on this night there are no insults. This is an evening for philosophy, light joking and Christmas verses. At some point in the evening, most of the musicians order a round of drinks for the house. Soon everyone is drunk -- a breach of etiquette on other occasions. There is an air of permissiveness toward younger, inexperienced singers, who are allowed to try their wings.

Established singers, especially the better ones, strive to maintain their self-control and perform with their usual expertise, so that their reputations will not suffer. A double tempo style known as the "Tra La Li La Tra La Le" is undertaken. This song has a chorus, unlike all other Maltese styles, and the extemporaneous leader part is taken in turn by almost everyone. There is no continuity except sentiment. Singing continues until dawn when everyone goes home for a few hours sleep before attending Morning Mass with their families.

INFORMAL OCCASIONS

In a very real sense, Maltese singers perform almost any time or place. Maltese women, washing clothes in their own courtyard, may sing to a neighbor. Serious folk music is more dependent upon the accidental meeting of singers and guitarists in any one of the thirty-some bars scattered over the islands. It is here that new singers practice, socialize and establish themselves; that new guitarists try their skills, and established musicians enjoy themselves. During the summer, musicians usually gather by the sea on weekends to enjoy the sun and water and singing with each other.

THE TRIUMPHAL TOUR

Yet another occasion for music in Malta is the triumphal tour, another version of *serata*. This phenomenon developed as the result of the record industry and involves a special invitation by a popular dance band manager, bar owner, or group of villagers issued to a singer or guitarist who has produced a successful record. Musicians will travel to the appointed place and sing for several hours, being provided with food and lodging if they have to leave the main island. The audience pays to enter, is more formal and less informed than many other audiences. Performance is on a stage; thus isolating the audience. In this context, some individuals may even ask musicians for their autographs. The musicians take these to be festive occasions, often staying out all night to have bull sessions, pillow fights, or to drink and socialize.

The musical occasion in Malta can be mapped. The examples given here represent a composite (made from many descriptions and personal observations) from which it is possible to arrive at either a simple listing, as above, or a more formal ranking.

ROUTES AND STRATEGIES

Far more attention has been given in the literature to rules and to a lesser extent to maps, than to routes and strategies. While it is true that routes and strategies may be seen as extensions of maps and rules, there is a distinct advantage to focusing upon those aspects of cognition. This is primarily true because cultural rules are simply instructions for constructing, combining, interpreting and manipulating symbols.

There are many choices to be made among rules, for rules are sometimes contradictory. It is in the superimposition of strategies and routes upon rules and, to a lesser extent upon maps, that leads to the clear realization of behavioral patterns within a human group.

There is a distinction to be made between strategies and routes, although the two areas are highly interrelated. Strategies can be seen as having to do with planning or managing activity, often through the use of consciously created, sometimes individualistic devices. In contrast, routes have to do with planning or managing in a more generalistic sense; that is, as a highway route is a course to be traveled, so in other areas of behavior a cognitive route is a frequently used, known course of action. A route is likely to be a cultural device, known to many, while a strategy may be highly individualistic.

Routes, as a course of action to be traveled, refer to strategies employed by individuals in past circumstances in a successful manner which have become generally accepted. Until recently, the route to success in American opera was to be found in the process of hard study, diligent work and successful appearances in Europe prior to working in America. The situation is now changing, but success in European theaters or opera houses is still a recognized means of acquiring a position in American opera companies.

As expressions of tradition, routes are not firmly bound into one specific course of action, nor is there any clear distinction to be made at this level between routes which are generally acceptable to society and those which are not. Some routes may be more acceptable than others, but even a route which is unacceptable to the vast majority of society is nevertheless potential and known; it is these two factors which will test and disclose the availability of a route.

In Malta, any woman who sings in public is regarded as a prostitute, whether she is or not. Therefore, any woman desiring to be a singer has a potential set of routes open to her: she may be a prostitute or not, although in any case she will be regarded as one if she sings in public. The association is traditional.

It has been mentioned before that Indri Brincat, the Maltese guitarist, so thoroughly broke the tradition that he created a totally new form. He developed it out of traditional material and slowly shifted his emphasis until improvisation broke the bonds that held the musical form stable. He then had to take the cultural consequences of his action.

It is claimed generally that Malta is a highly egalitarian society. In some cases, this is true. Each person feels himself to be inherently equal to any other, in spite of the presence of a status hierarchy. This is particularly true of musicians where policemen, grave-diggers, business men, electricians and lavatory attendants forget their distinctions while singing together.

Although it is obvious that some musicians are better than others, the musicians themselves refuse to verbalize this directly. Musicians are by nature permissive; fine performers allow small children to sing or play with them. The best singer will sing with the worst, and Mr. Brincat willingly plays guitar with visiting ethnomusicologists. Anyone may learn to sing; anyone may try; anyone may assess his own abilities as he wishes. The attitude is well conveyed by the Maltese proverb, "Whoever has a mouth to talk with, can say anything he likes".

In this egalitarian context, it would seem that innovation would be impossible, with high pressure to conform. This is generally true. If a person excels in any field, he immediately becomes the object of highly complex attacks and must run a gauntlet of envy and jealousy. If someone excels, his children may be scorned or slapped, and economically successful families suffer continuous thefts or high degrees of gossip. There is some belief that God takes vengeance upon the successful, and is expressed in the proverb, "If God gives you money, what else is He going to give you?"

169

This somewhat chilling Maltese atmosphere would seem to require tremendous ego-strength if one is innovative. In music, which is totally innovative by definition, a good musician needs genius, cunning, superiority and courage. To be a musician at all, one must possess an intense, burning passion for music. This quality is essential because of the pressure under which the creator is placed. Slander against good musicians is the norm, rather than the exception.

There are two sides to this problem. If one person is better at something than another, the reaction to this discovery is called *għajjur* (envy, jealousy). A jealous person feels a lack in him/herself when he/she sees the superiority of another, and it is believed that jealous people are not happy and die in misery. The true test of the presence of jealousy comes after death. The corpse excretes, but since this is a general characteristic of human corpses, the pervasiveness of the belief is apparent.

Jealousy, whether of musical superiority or another aspect of behavior, can take three cultural routes: witchcraft, rumor, or vengeance. With witchcraft, this is probably dealing with mythical statement, for no witches are known to exist on the island, yet all informants characterize their activities in the same terms. The witch hides his or her feelings from the people evoking jealousy and compliments the envied person extravagantly, while secretly making curses. These curses can be countered by the burning of olive leaves, the blessing of the house, or attaching pairs of bull horns in prominent places.

The second route, that of rumor, is more complex. Lies are told about people of ability. The majority of the authors' information about Maltese musicians took this form:

this singer left his wife after three days (actually, he has two sons by her, about six years' difference in age); that singer does not write his own ballads (yet, books of his songs exist); another singer betrayed his friends, and so forth.

The slander must occur outside the musical context to be the result of jealousy. There is always an accuser and an accused and the assumption is that the accuser feels himself to be of lesser ability than the accused. For this reason, scorn and slander are accepted with equanimity by most musicians; in effect, they are being complimented. Remembering that the compliment of the witch is regarded with grave suspicion, one can perceive a cultural model which is a reverse pecking order. The person best at his trade receives the most slander and enjoys the most honor, thereby. Thus, an insult is a form of compliment and a compliment is an insult.

The first two routes, witchcraft and rumor, involved internal action and are called "things of the heart". Both forms rebound on the jealous person and cause him or her great unhappiness. The third route, vengeance, is externalized and in this pattern, one individual physically injures another -- by scratching his car, stealing his guitar, or slapping his child. Apparently, musicians once chose this route for some time; fisticuffs were once common in Malta. Police action has put an end to this route and this may account for the present proliferation of rumors.

All three reactions to expertise apply only so long as one remains within reasonable bounds. In musical terms, this means that musicians who create within the normal forms will be subject to jealousy reactions. Mr. Brincat enjoys any passing rumor that comes his way as a mark of his adaptability into "correct" behavior.

There is yet another cultural route, designed to define the limits of conformity. This is the challenge, or *sfida*. It is rarely used, although everyone knows about it and there is much gossip about it. This is not, as in Western terms, a call to competition. It is a blow at the entire personality of an individual who has gone beyond acceptable limits. In the case of a musician, this could mean that not only his musicianship was in question, but also his very existence. Only one challenge was issued during the authors' stay in Malta, and that was to Indri Brincat. By the time it was issued, Mr. Brincat had moved so far out of the musical system that a reaction was to be expected. It came in the most agonizing of ways.

Mr. Brincat was extremely careful to maintain a distinction between folk and popular music. Although other musicians, wanting "fame" or a little extra money, would create a typical Maltese verse form which could be sung to a popular melody and recorded, Brincat flatly refused. He considered himself to be a traditional Maltese folk musician. However, Il-Fanfru, an older singer who had started late in life and was in a hurry to establish himself, arranged for someone else to write verses for him, then asked Brincat to accompany him on a record. Brincat agreed; contract arrangements were far advanced when it was learned that the melodies were not traditional. Brincat was greatly upset and asked to be released from the contract. Without a word, Il-Fanfru contracted another guitarist and Brincat cut off relations with Il-Fanfru.

There are two versions of this story. The one above is that of Brincat. The version of Il-Fanfru stressed his innocence in placing Brincat in this quandary, and the care he took to let him out of the contract before getting another guitarist. The challenge was clear. Here was a man who has progressed in innovation exclusively through the Maltese idiom until he began to burst its bounds. His music led him to alter the forms. But he was a folk guitarist, abhorring the idea of leaving his own tradition, in spite of the fact that he was the agent for change by virtue of his innovative genius.

It is also clear that Brincat imagined the challenge. This means that he knew he had gone beyond the limits of his tradition and was caught. If he was no longer a folk musician, what was he? Caught in the grip of his own progress, Brincat reacted. He began to berate his friends and cease to speak to them. He forced his opinions on his accompanist; one left him. He turned to outsiders for the comfort he needed so desperately. Arriving at the authors' house, knowing no English, he came just to play his guitar. Prevented by the ethic of non-interference in helping him across his barriers, the authors were in agony for the man. He ceased playing in public, pretending to repair his guitar and for weeks appeared only to play for contract arrangements.

In the meantime, he practiced, trying to move out of Maltese music to play popular music. He copied Spanish, Italian and other types of music while he poured out information to the authors on the nature of traditional Maltese style. His performances vacillated between highly traditional music, mediocre imitations of popular music and truly inspired progressions beyond his own systems. He no longer knew who he was.

In this state of mind, Brincat misinterpreted many signals from his fellow musicians. He had exceeded known cultural routes and had no strategy to protect himself. He finally faced himself and decided that of the options available to him, the only logical route for him to follow was to return to the general system. In order to remain within his tradition, he joined his worst enemies and began to play for Il-Fanfru and his friends.

Thus, the pressure of the tradition, in conflict with the requirement for constant innovation within it, was resolved in this case by total capitulation. Yet Brincat's capitulation was only apparently complete. He continued to display the appropriate public behavior and playing of many Maltese guitarists, but continued to improvise in private.

Brincat's action and choices in this matter represent strategies more than routes. In deciding to play publicly in a more accepted manner, while continuing his innovative activities at home, he created a plan and a device for managing his own public image and meshing it happily with his private goals and desires.

Strategies are not limited to reactions to given situations. They may represent plans created in an attempt to reach a future goal. In the highly innovative environment of Maltese singing, one must certainly have a personal strategy for creating a perfect four-line verse during the 30 to 40 seconds between one's opponent's response to the latest comment and one's own next verse. In order to respond quickly and well, one excellent musician stated that he always thought of the last two lines of a four-line verse first; in these lines, he placed the main message of his response to his opponent. The first two lines could then be filled in with introductory or padding material in order to create a perfect rhyme if necessary. Such a device was only one of many for managing a situation.

Both strategies and routes have great potential in revealing valuable information to the ethnomusicologist. Neither has received a great deal of attention in the past. It is hoped that the investigation of not only routes and strategies, but also maps and rules will lead to an ever-deepening understanding of the nature of that complex phenomenon known as music.

Absolutely essential to any informed investigation of cognitive domains is care in elicitation of data. It is extremely easy in the formulation of questions to indicate to the informant what kind of a response might be desired. All too often the informant, particularly if he or she is being paid, will provide answers which are calculated to be pleasing to the ethnomusicologist, whether they are true or not.

Another pitfall in elicitation is to assume either that the informants are ignorant or that they cannot talk about something; it would be better advice to assume that the researcher has formulated the wrong questions. In terms of interpretation or explanation of information elicited, it is very tempting to simply assume that the interpretation of a cognitive system is identical to that of the informants, when actually, there is no evidence to indicate that maps or rules have anything to do with the way others conceive of them.

VALUE JUDGMENTS

If music is regarded as a human process, arbitrarily defined and delimited by human beings, the idea of evaluation or qualification of experience is obviously central to any understanding of the nature of the production of music. As Merriam has pointed out:

> ...despite the enormous literature devoted to aesthetics, it is extremely difficult to discover precisely what an aesthetic is (1964:-259).

In speaking of value judgments, this includes that ill-defined area commonly called aesthetics; however, the use of the term "audience" conjures up sets of preconceived ideas which tend to lead Western scholars into dangerous depths of miscalculations in attempting to identify cross-cultural perception of emotional and intellectual experience.

In Western terms, aesthetics is often defined as the study of the beautiful or the perception of that which is good or beautiful. Apel suggests that "musical aesthetics is the study of the relationship of music to the human senses and intellect" (1969:14). Others feel that the aesthetic concerns sensuous more than conceptual data. The common definition regards aesthetics as the study of the beautiful.

According to Merriam, there are six factors which compromise the concept of the aesthetic in Western society: (1) psychic or psychical distance (Bullough, 1912); (2) manipulation of form for its own sake; (3) attribution of emotion-producing qualities to music conceived strictly as sound; (4) attribution of beauty to the art product or process; (5) purposeful intent to create something aesthetic; (6) presence of a philosophy of an aesthetic.

It is considered somewhat ethnocentric to follow Merriam's suggestion that "the problem is to attempt to ascertain whether this specific Western concept is re-duplicated in any societies other than our own" (1964:261). Instead,

176

it is suggested that not only is the term "aesthetic" potentially misleading, but that it represents an alteration of a direction of focus which might well prove unacceptable in the investigation of the music of the world.

McAllester uses the phrase "functional esthetic" is discussing the Western Apache:

> There is little esthetic discussion in our sense. Appreciation of a song is nearly always phrased in terms of understanding it -- of knowing what it is for. One or two informants did speak of preferring song with long choruses and short verses, since these are easier to learn, but the usual preference was for the important healing songs or the sacred songs in the puberty ceremony. This "functional esthetic" is found very widely among pre-literate peoples (1960:471-472).

This begins to approach what is meant by "value judgments", but presents a problem in that the material is simply left alone after the statement that the aesthetic is a functional one, which tends to dismiss the idea of any judgmental capability beyond the most rudimentary sort.

Kaeppler has arrived at what is perhaps the most useful definition of value judgments:

> ...art is defined as cultural forms
> that result from creative processes
> which manipulate movement,
> sound, or materials. Aesthetics is
> defined as ways of thinking about
> such forms (1971:175).

The aesthetic, viewed as ways of thinking, allows an approach to an area of consideration which is no longer confined to the good, the true and the beautiful. Instead, in discussing the ways of thinking about musical forms or other contexts, one is led into a more open and potentially exciting area of investigation.

Looked at from Kaeppler's point of view, aesthetics can be viewed as value judgments and value field. This raises a wider set of questions which, unlike the more restrictive concept of aesthetics, allows a definite approach to these aspects of music. Value judgments, being a general quality of human life, are made at each level of cognition. Some of these levels are musical; some are related to musical performance, but are only peripheral to the music performed.

The most profound value judgments about the nature of music are those general limitations on choice which each culture possesses. What an individual is allowed to hear may be profoundly influenced by basic cultural values which either circumscribe or direct that individual. Choices may be made for the entirety of a culture.

For example, the Catholic Church made a strenuous effort to restrict the performance of secular music in the Middle Ages. Whether this had any real influence on the performance of secular music is questionable; however, the attempt was made, representing a general view of music for that time which undoubtedly had some repercussions. Within the context of Catholicism, certain pieces of music and certain intervals in music were similarly restricted. The tritone was called the "Devil's Interval" and the mode containing it was banned in church music.

Equally repressive attempts were made in the 1950's and early 1960's to restrict what was heard on radio and juke boxes to those recordings controlled by certain criminal elements within the United States. Some prominent recording artists were suddenly not heard. Through bribes, certain disc jockeys were persuaded to play only those recordings which would bring a profit to those involved.

Cultural factors of a less pervasive type also influence what music is heard and accepted by the people of a culture. A particular type of music may be culturally valued because of nationalistic tendencies. It is commonplace in those societies which are changing rapidly that a point is eventually reached where the culture-bearers realize they are losing their traditions. In this context, what is left of a previous tradition will be over-valued in their eyes, whether the musical type is itself of equal value to others or not.

Wachsmann has pointed out for Uganda that performance types or genres which are being superseded are frequently highly-valued:

> This kind of idealization of an older style or styles fulfills the national aspiration, in a musical sense...I failed completely to find anyone who said, "Oh, this is old

stuff", although everyone knew it was old stuff, and on the way out. And this is an interesting situation, because one would have to investigate carefully and clearly what was actually superseding what (1976:195-196).

The opposite may also happen, particularly in societies where the superseded form is still frequent. Among the Merina, for instance, there are two versions of stage presentation for folk music: the *hira-gasy* theater, and that which is simply called "theater". *Hira-gasy* is a staged presentation of long moral stories sung by eight singers, accompanied by a small orchestra. This form carries basic cultural values through their exposition in song. Theater, on the other hand, is fully Europeanized; the usual version is similar to Vaudeville. Musicians take "turns" on the stage; other tribes are degraded in song through caricatures of their music; comics and straight-men make their appearance on stage.

These two forms are both available as theater in large cities. The *hira-gasy* audience is composed mainly of older men and women interested in the moral questions propounded by the singers, while theater is the venue of the young. Here, the performance is toward the more modern stage presentations and the older style is devalued.

Value judgments of a non-musical nature may reflect class performance as well. Among the Maltese, members of the upper class rarely listen to Maltese folk music, preferring imported Italian forms instead. Their rationale for this is the myth that folk singers are always fighting. They raise horrid images of guitarists breaking guitars over singers' heads in scruffy bars, repeating mythical stories about recent incidents of extreme violence. In truth, singers fight with words, not fists.

Here, the upper class is reacting, at least partly, to the close association among musicians, homosexuals, prostitutes and racetrack touts. Folk musicians are an out-group for the upper class. What they are avoiding is not the music, but the setting of the music.

The introduction of Christianity has generally meant the death-knell of many older forms associated with religion. Traditional ritual performances are often avoided by Christian-ized members of a community. As a result, older musical styles which have been associated with non-Christian ritual and are now viewed as "sinful", may die out for lack of an audience.

Physical factors may also limit the public's participation in a particular place for, or type of, music. The Albert Hall in London is one of the major concert halls of the city. Many devotees of classical music refuse to go there, because the hall is a whispering gallery and performances are often ruined if one is seated in the wrong place. Performances there may relegate a specific performer to a special kind of oblivion in London.

Many people also suffer from a physical inability to listen to certain kinds of music. Men are especially prone to difficulty with high sounds, and it is common for men to say they prefer not to listen to opera because sopranos hurt their ears.

Aside from those value judgments based on factors

which are totally non-musical, there are a number of cases where value judgments are only partially musical. This is especially noticeable when one tries to deal with the concept of the "best man". It was once axiomatic in the study of folk music that the first task of the scholar was to seek out the "best man" and make recordings of him in preference to other musicians. Unfortunately, many cultures have value judgments about musicians which relate not so much to their being the best performer, but rather the "proper" performer. "Best man" is a value judgment about the nature of the musician as well as the music. The "best man" is a consequence of Western tradition; however, a full understanding of the music of any society requires a study of the range of competence of various musicians within a style or genre.

This becomes especially crucial in those areas where the "proper man" in a specific performance is not necessarily the "best man" to perform, in musical terms. Mention has been made above that in Tikopia the concept of "expert" (*purotu*) implies that some performers of music and dance are better than others. At the same time, noblemen frequently function as "experts" not by reason of their musical ability, but because they are the only "proper persons" to sing or dance in certain ceremonial circumstances. An element of Tikopian politeness also enters into the situation. When a nobleman attends a dance, his social position brings attention as it would in any other situation. As experts are normally found to the fore in dancing and singing, chiefs who attend dances are usually given the position of expert, whether they are expert or not.

Behague points out that in Candomble drumming, the master drummer is regarded as the "best man". This is the result not of quality of his performance so much as his knowledge of repertoire. Master drummers are confirmed and thereby socially recognized as having reached a certain level of competence which is only partially musical (1976:-200).

Draper has pointed out that social recognition may not coincide with experiences:

> Last summer, I went back to the Choctaw Indian Reservation to get all the variants that I could of a particular genre. When I had been there previously, there was a "best man" for the Choctaws, but when I got back last summer, he was too old. He had forgotten the variants of a number of varieties of songs. But he had maintained the social role as best singer (1976:203).

While it is clear that cultural and physical tendencies may intermesh with musical value judgments, there are yet some areas in which music is judged by itself. The problem here is methodological: In what way may the investigator get at value judgments about music? The authors agree with Merriam who states that not all societies express their judgments concerning music in the same way. The concepts of "good" and "bad" do not always apply. In what ways, then, do societies express themselves in this area?

One common factor seems to be the use of native cognitive categories about other things. In Madagascar, singers who are regarded as having truly great voices are described as having "blue" voices. "Blueness" is the quality of sacredness, as seen in such combinations of *bazomanga* (blue tree) which is the sacred tree of the circumcision ceremony of the Sakalava; or *Ambohimanga* (Blue Mountain), the name for the sacred fortified village of the Merina where the remains of the great king Andrianampoinimerina are buried. The quality of "blueness" relates to excellence in singing because of the association between Heaven and the sky, which is blue.

The same is true of the Cherokee "straight" voice. The quality which makes a voice good is the ability to reach the spirits in a straight line. This value judgment slides over into value judgments about the quality of a voice.

Among the Maltese, the situation is somewhat different. The aim of the Maltese singer is to sing above his range and the most valued voice type is a high tenor. Thus, the description of a fine voice is usually phrased, "He sings like a woman", which expresses the complex of ideas about the proper voice type.

Another way of indicating a fine Maltese performance is gestural, rather than verbal. When a singer or guitarist has done a fine job, members of the listening audience will either raise the thumb of the right hand and jerk the hand straight up in the air, or, holding all fingers extended, slash straight down through the air. This gesture is closely related to the concept *sewwa* (truth). That which is true in Maltese is also right or correct; the gesture indicates the "rightness" of a performance. Also in the same cognitive set is the concept *ezatt* (exact). Truth, correctness and exactness are all qualities of a fine performance. While the verbalizations can be elicited out of context, in context the vertical gesture is used.

One of the reasons for the lack of verbalizations about expertness in Malta lies in the necessity not to compliment anyone to his face. As mentioned before, a compliment is an insult in Malta, since witches are said to compliment those of whom they are jealous. Verbal comments about a performance which are phrased in direct language could easily be misinterpreted.

It is possible, however, to compliment a performer by insulting him. In the playback of a particularly fine recording session of a group of musicians, the authors' interpreter became enthusiastic about the recording and said, "That was a terrible recording!" Cultural values made it impossible to compliment on competence in a direct manner; indirection, therefore, must be the rule.

In spite of the difficulties involved, the Maltese have a complex, flexible means of defining the relative competence of a performer. This system is based on naming devices. In Malta, there are very few surnames and as a result, many people have the same name. In the village of Marsaxlokk, for instance, there were six men named Carmenu Bugejja. In a small alley in the village of Zabbar, there were two men named John Scicluna among ten households. In order to avoid confusion, it is necessary to use nicknames as another naming device.

Naming devices take several forms. One may be known by first name plus surname; by nickname alone; by first name plus nickname; by first name plus name of village; by surname only; or in cases of dire necessity, by first name plus surname, plus nickname.   Each individual may be named differentially for clarity in different situations. The musicians use these naming devices as a means of indicating the relative competence of performers.

In order to clarify the naming system, here is the same name of a single individual with all its variants: Anthony Borg (not a real singer), is nicknamed *in-Nabbu* (the sparrow); lives in the village of Zejtun. Depending upon his current situation, he could be called Anthony, Borg, Anthony Borg, *in-Nabbu*, Tony *in-Nabbu*, or Tony *taz-Zejtun*.

Fine singers are few. There are two ways in which one may recognize the category of highest excellence. One may say that a man is a singer (*ghannej*) rather than an amateur or listener (*dilettant*). This separates the few great singers and guitarists from all others. One may also identify a truly great musician by using the formula of the first name plus nickname (Tony *in-Nabbu*). The entire evaluation system is listed in the following chart:

Evaluation by Naming

Master singer, leader Master guitarist	Tony *in-Nabbu*
Fine singer or guitarist	*in-Nabbu*
Fair singer	Tony, Anthony
Barely acceptable singer, or accompanying guitarist	Borg
Bad musician	Anthony Borg, Tony
Returned emigrants who are not yet in the system	Tony *taz-Zejtun*

This system of evaluation of competence has two main values for the Maltese. First, the use of the naming device instead of a qualifying statement allows people to indicate their feelings about one another within the hearing of the individual being spoken of. In this way, each singer may know his place in the system in the mind of every other. In addition, the system is flexible. If the singer has done a poor job on a given evening, he may find himself referred to by a nickname one or two categories down the list from normal.

A singer's status in any one of these categories is momentary and depends entirely on the relative evaluation of the speaker. As a young singer gets better, he may well move up in the system. Older singers may move down as they become less able to sustain the frantic pace.

A striking example is that of *il-Bies*, a blind singer who was once considered to be one of the greatest musicians on the islands. In 1969, he was always referred to as Pawlu *il-Bies* if past action was discussed; but simply as *il-Bies* if present action was discussed. One singer said of him, "Now he's getting very old and his mind is going. He is not the man he once was." The blind singer's fortunes changed, however. In 1972, he had recovered status; clearer thinking was indicated in his performance and he was once more referred to as Pawlu *il-Bies*.

The last category, that of outsider, refers to those people who are an unknown quantity. As an example, Zarenu Ellul went to Australia for a number of years. Upon his return, he settled in the village of Tarxien and attempted to enter a musicians' group. When he was an unknown quantity, he was referred to as "Zarenu from Tarxien". Two years later, he had moved in status and was then known as "Zorru", a short form of Zarenu.

The elicitation of evaluative judgments concerning the relative competence of musicians in the system is not yet well advanced. This may lie in one of two factors. While many ethnomusicologists have realized that each culture has its own way of verbalizing evaluative judgments, some of these ways are exceedingly indirect and complex, and not easily elicited.

The second factor is that some scholars still do not believe that systems of folk music have an aesthetic component, and so refuse to look for evaluative statements. This may also lie in the fact that value judgments concerning music are so frequently stated negatively. The negative statement of values so common in Western society can easily be used as a means of determining the grounds upon which a value system rests. Negative statements about performances of types of music will be found at all cognitive levels.

It is common in our own society to be told, "I don't like Country and Western music; but I think Willie Nelson is just great." Such comments indicate that, while the class "Country and Western music" is not appreciated by the listener, one individual within the category does have qualities which are favored. In such situations, many people may say that their favorite singer isn't really a Country and Western singer at all. This tendency may be viewed as the statement that a particular musician transcends the type of music in which he or she is normally placed.

Similarly, an individual may express a lack of tolerance for an entire category of music, such as "I don't like the modern American interpretation of Beethoven". Many musicians trained during the time of Toscanini find the modern interpretation of Beethoven somewhat unsettling. Wachsmann mentions a similar reaction:

> ...I went through this experience when I first heard Schubert Lieder sung in English by English singers. I felt like emigrating straight away again. But I did realize, as time went on, that I had a tradition that I valued very highly...I began to accept that there is an English way of singing Schubert Lieder in English (1976:221-222).

The underlying canons or rules for making music may also be stated as value judgments concerning specific performances. This usually takes the form, "he made a mistake". The breaking of musical rules is often verbalized. It is common to hear someone say that they will not attend the local symphony because the violins don't play in tune. This is the expression of a rule of competence because, for performers to be competent in Western society, they must play in tune.

Other societies express themselves in a similar way. In the *spirtu pront* style in Malta, the improvised verse of four lines must rhyme with the end of lines two and four. Furthermore, the rhyming must not force the grammar; this is a primary rule. When an individual makes a mistake, the gossip is immediate and his relative position in the evaluation system goes down. Other rules are less strict. For instance, the best verse is in Latin syllable structure: 8, 7, 8, 7. While this is the ideal, singers who include more or fewer syllables in their lines are not regarded as bad singers; but they will never be regarded as great singers unless they learn how to create verses of perfect syllable structure.

In Malta, there are 37 "mistakes" in singing and guitar playing which are fundamental to the system. Yet other, more complex rules are known only to fine singers and guitarists. All but one of these rules can be checked out in performance. The ineffable rule known only to singers is, "If you think up a verse and then forget it in that instant before you are to sing and are forced to make up another verse to replace it, it is a mistake".

Using the basic rules or canons of music-making in Malta, singers assess one another's individual performances in terms of correctness. What is being discussed here is competence. A truly great singer or guitarist is one who is able to go beyond competence to that transcendent quality which, in the Euro-American tradition, is labeled the aesthetic. However, consistent adherence to the rules is the mark of a very fine singer.

Preferences between opposing items in the same realm may indicate style changes as well as preferences. In Madagascar, there are two types of tube zither. The tube zither is made of a large bamboo with an internode at least two feet long. In one style of *valiha*, the strings are fashioned by slitting the outer bark of the bamboo from one node to another in two parallel lines, then carefully cutting the outer bark away from the inner. Bridges are placed beneath the now free string to tune it, and the ends are kept from splitting past the nodes by tying them with cord.

In the other type, metal strings made from telephone

cable are attached to the bamboo with nails, with splitting prevented by wrapping the node with a slice of tin can appropriately nailed down. These two types of strings have completely different qualities; the first is the older type, but the carrying power of the metal strings is deemed much greater. In addition, the tone is clearer since the slight irregularities in the bark of the bamboo can cause the string to be untrue.

Similarly, change has taken place in Tikopia in respect to a number of the less common dance types. This becomes more apparent at the *feasinga*, the larger daytime dance festivals given by the chiefs. Support for the chiefs at the *feasinga* is apparently not as strong as it was formerly. This seems to be related to the type of dances performed there and the preferences of the young people. In one case in 1952, young people absented themselves from the dancing of a *tusoko*, saying that they did not care for it:

> They say it's a lazy dance; they like their bodies to sway in the dance. Their desire is for *matav-aka*, (canoe-bow dance). They hold that they are not skilled -- that they are skilled in *matavaka*. That is their desire (Firth, field notes, 1952:xiv, 15).

On another occasion in 1952, all four chiefs came to a *feasinga* but only about 15 dancers appeared and it was finally abandoned. One of the men gave Firth a lecture on how the younger generation no longer supported their chiefs. Here is a case in which both personal preferences and changes in the system are involved in the value judgment.

191

The *matavaka* is the popular dance among the young people. Other, more formal dances are usually found at the daytime festivals and do not appeal to the young people. In Tikopia, the right to absent one's self is a form of protest; but it is difficult to decide what the young people were protesting. Did they object to the dances, or to the *feasinga*, itself?

Negative statements also occur in cases when a person has committed him/herself to a particular category of music, but finds fault with a performance within that category. This is perhaps the most interesting area for study. This negative evaluation of specific performances is one of the most valuable tools in the determining of those qualities of the performance which give it value for the listeners.

While it may seem negative statements concerning music have been dwelt on, it is obvious that positive statements occur. In Malta, fine singers have avid supporters who follow them from performance to performance, often armed with tape recorders to capture the moment of their latest triumph. One such man has a tape library covering over twenty years of recording.

The enthusiasm of listeners and singers alike is described by the same Maltese term, *dilettant*. These are the lovers of the art who follow it either as singers or as listeners. To be a *dilettant* is not as good as being an *ghannej* (singer), but it is a status within the system. The passion for music in Malta is expressed by the word *namur*, which translates best into English as "intense love".

This concept of following given performers as well as styles is present in Western society as well. While statements of this kind are not aesthetic in the normal sense of the word, they do indicate that a value judgment has been made and that certain expectations have been set up which the individual wishes to repeat.

The question of expectation has not been well investigated in the study of music; though it is clear that each person who responds to music develops certain expectations. If one performer or a group of performers fulfills those expectations better than others, one frequently expresses that preference in terms of individuals or styles or genres rather than in more general terms.

Styles of music within the same society may differ widely from one another in terms of value and opinion. In Malta, one element of music is valued over another in both the *spirtu pront* and the *bormliza*. In the *spirtu pront*, it is the poetry and wit of the singer which is important; voice type is secondary. In the *bormliza*, voice type is most highly valued, for if a singer cannot create his or her own verses, someone will "feed" them lines. Each style has its own rationale within the system.

Such varied judgments are fairly typical of musical systems where different styles of genres exist. While a general statement could be made for music, differential emphases usually occur at the level of style. This may be why it is so difficult to define music in any given society. While the qualities of value in music may be stated in any particular instance, emphasis of one quality over another may be common.

Up to this point, those aspects of value judgments about music which relate to the concepts of competence and expectations within styles have been discussed. Attention is now turned to that area of musical performance in which verbalizations no longer serve a reasonable purpose. Until now, it has been possible to describe value judgments about music as "fit". The performers lived up to the expectations of the style; they were competent. This concept of "fit" (competence, or correctness) will suffice only so far. There are yet other cases where, when the expectations of the individual come together with the real performance, something beyond mere acceptance of competence occurs. Expectations can be either achieved or transcended and, if transcended, they become exceedingly difficult to verbalize.

What is the nature of the expectation of an audience or other performers when dealing with this area of judgment? There are two possibilities. Either the culture has taught individuals that they may at some time meet an unexpectedly beautiful performance with which they cannot cope in normal times; or performers may be viewed as individuals walking a special kind of tightrope, in which disaster is always a possibility. The first concept is familiar. The second may explain why performances have such a quality of excitement about them. As Fernea has put it:

> ...in a sense, every performance is like the daring young man on the flying trapeze. There has to be that element of possibility that the violin will hit a wrong note, that the ballerina will fall off her toe-shoe...It's the feeling that suddenly the person is transformed from prima ballerina, from Giselle, dancing her heart out, to a human being who's suddenly twisted her

> ankle. It's that sudden loss of
> illusion, that sudden recognition
> that the man is just like me, he's
> forgotten his line, that's what I'd
> do if I were standing up there. It
> seems to me that this is the kind
> of risk that sustains attention, and
> then your audience becomes re-
> laxed and convinced as the per-
> suasive professionalism of the
> performers manage to remove his
> doubt, and it becomes more and
> more comfortable (1976:156).

Fernea implies that the potential for risk is an attractive quality of performance. It is certainly true in the case of music, where all musical styles involve special skills and often great complexity for correct performance. The performer is a risk-taker; risking a failure with every performance. This is true even in societies without fine art musics.

The attractiveness of music may well lie in its very difficulty. Many would-be musicians fail to achieve compe-tence and remarkable performances are infrequent. This points out a quality of performance which has not been mentioned before. Where specific performance tasks are not communally shared, the performers of various specific roles such as music-making are demonstrating *difference*. They are saying in effect, "I am doing what you cannot or do not do and I am displaying it back to you". This sense of difference may lie in the complexity -- the risk-taking -- involved in the creation of an art.

Up to this point, concern has been with those instances

where the major aspect of value judgments is competence; now concern is with those cases where performance transcends competence. This is what is more usually conceived of as an aesthetic experience, involving the sudden realization that a performance has reached an ideal which was often unmanifested before it was demonstrated.

In such cases, it is frequently impossible to verbalize the experience well. There are many examples and the following quote from King is typical:

> There was a performance on Mozart's birthday by the Budapest (string quartet) in New Orleans. The Budapest got carried away, and so did the audience. And it wasn't the Budapest any more. Everything and everyone was involved in the performance -- the hall, the audience, the musicians -- and suddenly there was Mozart. But Mozart wasn't there where you could point. I'm not a trained musician, but I could see it (1976:224).

The uncommon, transcendent performance is often approached in this way. Verbalizations fail. Where verbalizations fail, the means by which people express their feelings is lacking and may take the form of "inappropriate" behavior.

For example, when Judith Anderson toured in the English translation of "Medea" in the late 1940's, McLeod was present at the performance in Salt Lake City. The audience was startled into the realization that the performance was transcendent and when the curtain descended on the last act, there was total silence in the auditorium. No one applauded. After a time, the curtain rose and Judith Anderson stood in the center of the stage; the silence continued. Anderson broke the mood by saying, with tears in her voice, "Thank you. Thank you very much". She then gave an extremely theatrical, nineteenth-century stage bow, as much to say, "This was a performance and I was the performer". At this point, the audience stood up and screamed; and after a while, they began to applaud. Both silence and screaming are inappropriate behavior in a theater, and here, where the performance was too excellent to perceive properly, the audience reacted with behavior which did not fit.

In Malta, the authors asked their major informant what he would do if he ever encountered such a performance. He said, "I would go to the man and shake his hand". This, too, is somewhat inappropriate behavior, although it is not verbal and does not break the verbal canons for indirectness, it does extend the usual gesture of up-and-down approval to direct contact across space. He would be breaking another canon -- that of allowing performers to have empty space around them.

This canon of atypical response to atypical performance may help one to understand why such experiences are rarely verbalized. While little has been written on the state of mind involved in such experiences, it is clearly a change of consciousness. Victor Turner (1967, 1969) has emphasized the concept of "communitas" -- a direct, immediate, communal experience of oneness in which an individual senses, if only for an instant, a merging of his consciousness with all of mankind. While communitas is frequently associated with religion, it may also be a part of the experience of meeting or listening to music. Mihaly Csikszentmihalyi has recently suggested a term which is in many ways related to communitas -- "flow".

"Flow" is a state in which one's actions follow one another according to an internal logic which apparently needs no conscious intervention on the part of the individual. It is a unified feeling of flowing from one moment to the next, in total control, with little distinction being made between the self and the environment, between past, present and future. Wachsmann is speaking of this state when he says:

> I'm very conscious when my bowing is labored, and I am equally conscious when it comes perfectly natural and right. It runs by itself (1976:234).

McAloon and Csikszentmihalyi indicate six elements for distinctive features of the flow experience. These are:

(1) The experience of merging action and awareness, for there is no sense of duality present during "flow". An individual is very aware of what he is doing; however, he cannot be aware of being aware of what he is doing, since if he is, there will be a break in cognition and a resulting self-consciousness which will make him stumble.

(2) The merging of action and awareness results in and is made possible by a centering of attention on a limited area of action or thought. Hence, consciousness is narrowed, intensified and focused.

(3) The individual experiences a loss of ego as he/she is immersed in the "flow" of an experience. The suggestion is made that the self is forgotten during the experience, but this does not mean a loss of self-awareness, since when the "flow" experience is broken, recollection of the experience will produce increased consciousness.

(4) A person "in flow" is in control of his/her actions and the environment. That is, skills are matched precisely to the demands made by the action.

(5) There is usually a coherent, non-contradictory set of demands for action which provide clear feedback to a person's actions. That is, there are explicit rules for action which make the evaluation of action in retrospect and the action, itself, easy and unproblematic.

(6) "Flow" is intrinsic. There seems to be no requirement for any kind of reward outside of the activity itself (McAloon and Csikszentmihalyi, 1975).

Along with the ideas involved in "flow", it is possible to consider another level of analytic awareness about the types of cognition usually dealt with in musical settings. With refinement, the idea of "flow" may indeed prove helpful in ethnomusicology.

When a student is learning to play an instrument, to sing or to dance, it is necessary that his or her attention be fully focused on the mechanics of learning. Later, as these physical skills improve, it is possible to concentrate on other factors. If a style has been fully learned, it then becomes possible to "flow" with the experience of making music, as it is possible to "flow" with the experience of participating in music as part of the audience.

Several years ago, Herndon and McLeod made a recording for a pianist who was applying for a Fulbright fellowship. In the course of the recording experience, the pianist, who knew all his material quite well, began communicating directly with his instrument and "flowing". There was a lack of consciousness of time passing; all those present in the recital hall became aware participants in a moving experience.

"Flow" is an intimate experience of performers. Once competence has been achieved, the pleasure of performing lies mainly in this quality. Here, the mind is freed of the necessity to be totally involved in simply producing the effect. The overarching sense of control over performance is such that some of the attention can then be diverted from mere mechanics. In such moments, the performer can move into a new awareness of the piece being performed which is transcendent of self and one's formal view. Where group performance is involved and all are competent, the concept of oneness in the entire performing group, of "communitas", takes over. In these circumstances, an orchestra may suddenly become a living organism.

Another kind of cognition at a very general level has not been discussed in the literature, but might be called "flash". This is the opposite, in many ways, of "flow". In "flash", there is an intensification of awareness of the entire environment, a consciousness of the importance of the moment and a need to mark it in some way. It has been said with some validity that all Americans who were old enough to be aware of the importance of the event can probably say quite easily where they were and what they were doing when President Kennedy was assassinated. This event, totally unexpected, was of such importance that it was almost burned into the awareness of all.

In musical terms, it is not unusual for an individual to have had one or two experiences in which "flash" has occurred. A guest on a late night television talk show, for example, noted that his environment on first hearing "Ode to Billy Joe" on the radio was etched firmly into his mind. He recalled with great clarity the traffic intersection at which he was stopped when the song began; the people, the buildings, the odors, the external sounds; all were present in his mind and in some way were connected to his experience.

It might be said that every time people attend a musical event or occasion, they have a certain mental ideal against which the actual performance is matched with certain expectations, which may or may not be fulfilled by the performance, itself. However, the general expectation is that the ideal will not be fully achieved, although it may be approached closely. When the ideal actually does merge with the moment, a sense of "flash" takes place, resulting in unusual behavior patterns.

As in the case of Kennedy's assassination, the awful potential, the unexpected, occurs. Thus, the "flash" experience will take place either as a result of a totally unexpected event, or the achievement of an unexpected degree of perfection in a marked event.

Like "flow", "flash" may take place either for a performer or for a listener. It may be a communal experience or an individual one. One type of "flash" is not reasonable for a performer, but occurs among listeners. This is the state of mind in which the attention is so firmly focused on what is happening that the rest of the environment blanks out, and the listener is totally unconscious of everything else. In circumstances of this kind, the listener may be immobilized, with arms and legs ceasing to function. Another common concomitant of this state is the raising of the hair on the back of the neck, the tingling of the scalp and other indications of psychic shock. This state of mind may last for some time after the performance is finished, and may explain the silence of the audience at the performance of "Medea".

There is a "flash" experience in which time is shifted or becomes meaningless into a psychological "now", as Wachsmann puts it. Unlike those occasions in which the environment is burned into the awareness, in this variety, the environment is excluded and concentration is only upon the object or performance. After such an experience, one tends to babble, and again, there are no words to express what has happened. In this case, the atypical behavior is the inability to speak about it.

In all of these cases where transcendence of competence occurs, the states of mind are abnormal and behavior is often atypical. It is not surprising that people often phrase this as being "lifted out of one's self" or "transported". Some of the states of mind which occur in connection with religious experiences may differ slightly from the Western aesthetic experience, but they share the characteristic of the emergence of a changed state of awareness. This seems to be commonplace in association with music. Music is cognitively perceived in the ultimate sense, but it also seems to have the characteristic of changing perception in some way.

CONCLUSION

In this section, the ways in which music, which is primarily aural, is classified and evaluated by the mind were discussed. This is perhaps the most difficult area of all to assess correctly. Elicitation of data concerning the way in which music is viewed, evaluated, classified and experienced is one of the lesser explored areas in the study of music. Music is clearly subject to cultural factors here; but it is also a mark of the individual experience, both for performer and listener. As such, the data elicited are often contradictory and confusing. It is probably for this reason that so little has been said on this subject.

The purpose in this chapter has been to discuss some of the specific ways in which the problems of cognition and aesthetics can be approached. It is not enough to say that music is found in culture, for this approach is too broad, too all-encompassing. It lacks a sense of purpose and definition.

The specific examples given here are by no means to be regarded as the only ways in which to approach these more delicate and diffuse problems. Instead, they are offered as both concepts and discoveries of the authors. It is to be hoped that further study in this area will re-define many, if not most, of the principles discussed here.

6

THOUGHTS AND PROSPECTS

All through the planning, writing and reading of this book, there are several questions, assumptions and implications lying unanswered, like threads waiting to be gathered together into a tapestry. It is to these thoughts and prospects that we now turn our attention.

QUESTIONS

Throughout this book, the authors have sought to raise a number of different kinds of questions. In some cases, tentative answers have been proposed or boundaries suggested. For other questions, answers must await further research.

Perhaps the most important questions are those which can really never be answered, such as -- why do people make music? If the definition of music is not made too narrow, it soon becomes apparent that all human groups have something which might be called music. In some cases, this music is functionally for the same purpose, cross-culturally. In other cases, music is found to serve unique structural purposes for a given group.

Whatever the case, the extremely wide distribution of musical phenomena throughout the world has led many people to muse, to ponder, and to begin to investigate for themselves this elusive, complex and diverse human activity.

Ethnomusicologists seem compelled, from time to time, to quest for universals of music in an attempt to address this most basic "why" of their field of study.

Subjectively, it is probable that as long as there have been aware human beings acting, behaving, thinking and living in groups, there have probably been those among them who mused, reflected, and wondered why people were engaged in particular activities or why they held certain beliefs. Music is no exception to this type of questioning, as is evidenced by the vast number of origin and explanatory myths for music found throughout the world.

Objectively, the appearance of specialists who attempted to systematize, to compare cross-culturally the wide range of human activity called music is a fairly recent phenomenon. These specialists seem to have arisen out of Western culture, primarily, and for reasons which are not clear.

The observations, examinations and speculations concerning the question, "Why do people make music?" must remain elusive, for this is a question which cannot be directly approached. Instead, it must be approached indirectly.

Researchers usually find themselves asking not "*Why?*" but "*How* do people make music?" How do they think about it -- classify it -- theorize about it? How does the participation in, or listening to, music affect the physiology? How does music relate to narrative, myths, belief systems, or basic values? How do musical systems interact, compare or contrast with other cultural systems?

Through this kind of questioning, and through meticulous and systematic ethnographic descriptions of musical systems, it is thought possible to accumulate a data bank large enough to allow more objective approaches to the underlying question of "Why do people make music?"

Another underlying question -- although probably not of the same magnitude as the first -- is the question, "Why do people study ethnic musics?" That is, why do people worry about, think about, probe into why people make music? What kind of people are they -- where do they come from -- what is their background -- and what is their intention?

Ethnomusicology, the cover term under which those who study ethnic musics work, is, itself, very unclear and ephemeral. There is no agreement among those calling themselves ethnomusicologists as to whether ethnomusicology is a discipline, a field of study, or simply a helpful adjunct to other fields.

The training of ethnomusicologists has been, and continues to be, diverse. Most of the scholars currently operating in the field of ethnomusicology come from many different backgrounds and few people hold advanced degrees specifically in ethnic music. Of those who do, their training, points of view, and self-conceptualizations range over a vast territory, indeed. Perhaps the only common ground for those found under the umbrella of ethnomusicology is a certain amount of curiosity about music other than their own, a tendency toward involvement in active participation in some kind of music, itchy feet, and the tendency to rebel against established norms and disciplines.

There are those who devote a lifetime, both professionally and personally, to the exclusive study of music. There are others whose profession and employment lie elsewhere, who may be equally devoted to specific aspects of the study of ethnic music. Also, there are those who have only a passing interest in ethnomusicology, yet nevertheless manage to provide valuable insights to the pool of knowledge in this area.

Perhaps the best answer to the question, "Why do people study ethnic music?" is a very simple one -- because they want to. In some instances because of some compelling force, they *must* study musics other than their own. For others, the level of involvement may be transitory, minimal, or highly specific.

The question, "Why do people study ethnic music?" raises yet another question -- "*who* studies ethnic music?" Embedded in this latter question are historical trends and assumptions as well as theoretical implications. Historically, ethnomusicology has been synonymous with the study of "exotic" music and tied into the Western intellectual framework. For various complex reasons, the trend was toward working with music other than one's own.

The assumption was made that ethnomusicology necessarily involved observation and/or participation from an outsider's -- rather than an insider's -- point of view. Music might be seen as a keyhole through which one could view an entire society, or as an entity easily isolated and studied apart from its contexts. In either case, the scholar was tacitly assumed to have superior abilities to analyze, categorize, generalize, normalize and compare.

Yet, a contrary assumption has been applied to ethnomusicologists who were, themselves, "ethnic". Not all scholars who study music come from Western cultures, and it might be logically assumed that they would be encouraged to turn their attention toward Western music or to other (to them) "exotic" musics. This was not the case. For these non-Western scholars, pressure was applied to study their own musics, the assumption being that, for them, ethnomusicology necessarily involved observation and/or participation from an insider's -- rather than from an outsider's -- viewpoint.

Leaving any implications of paternalism, cultural superiority, or simple short-sightedness aside in considering these two contradictory assumptions, a methodological question remains. What are the advantages and disadvantages of studying music from outside? From inside? This is obviously an area crying out for further consideration, and one that may well be informed by previous and current experience within the discipline of anthropology.

Aside from who studies music and from what stance, one major question ought to be articulated -- "*How* should music be studied?" The preceding chapters constitute, for the authors, part of their answers to this question. In all fairness, however, it should be pointed out that the authors' answers are not the only answers. There are those who have widely divergent views, in terms of both theory and method.

In the final analysis, though, answers to these questions

really do not matter. What does matter is that this is an area open to all comers, a realm whose parameters are as yet uncharted, whose questions are as yet little understood, and whose promise for the understanding of human behavior is great.

This very openness, not only of the area of ethnomusicology, but also of its practitioners, explains better than anything else the reasons why an introductory text must maintain a professional level, without the expectation that the reader will necessarily devote full time and energy to the pursuit of ethnic music in any way. Instead, this is an area in which everyone can potentially make contributions. It is hoped that through an understanding of the rigorous approaches to ethnic music, former excesses of both zeal and ethnocentrism can be avoided.

ASSUMPTIONS

It has been a basic assumption throughout this book that music exists *as* culture, rather than *in* culture. To those new to the field, this may at first appear to be a minor assumption of little consequence; however, this is decidedly not the case.

If it is thought that music exists *in* culture, there is an immediate temptation to remove it from culture, to transport it to the sanctity of the laboratory and to dissect it in a scientific manner. Bluntly, if music is *in* culture, logic dictates that it can be taken *out* of culture. Conversely, if music is a thoroughly integrated aspect of culture, a different attitude is called for. New kinds of questions emerge, methodology changes, and interpretation is both broadened and deepened. The authors have a decided preference for music *as* culture.

In assuming that music *as* culture is a desirable point of departure, it is not assumed that all custom, group relations, or behavior will be necessarily germane to our study. Intensive, detailed, systematic observation does not imply exhaustive, all-encompassing data gathering. Selection is necessary.

Instead, the assumption is that the ethnomusicologist is free to circumscribe a field of concentration, depending on what research goals have been established. He or she may want to study a particular instrument, group, genre, song, ensemble, set of relationships, or domain of activities, which is only part of a larger and more complex social field. Or the goal may be a large and comparative one.

Whatever the focus of a single study may be, we assume that the aim of ethnomusicology, in congruence with all scientific endeavor, is to seek the simplest possible explanation of complex facts. These complex interrelationships must be fully set within a reasonably delimited, but flexible, context.

Yet another underlying assumption regarding this book and the field of ethnomusicology is the recognition of, and salute to, the fact that music is performed. Whether a specific human group has aural music orally transmitted or aural music transmitted in written form, all music is performed. Thus, the areas of kinesics, performance and context each play an extremely important role in the apprehension of musical phenomena and thinking about music. That is, it is human beings who make music, think about it, hear it and learn it. It is also human beings who study music, dealing with a sound process which takes place in time, in space and in consciousness.

In many ways, this recognition of the importance of the performance of music represents a serious departure from trends of thought within Western musical scholarly circles. There, the tendency has been to treat music as a thing instead of a process, resulting in different kinds of questions and assumptions regarding the preservation of materials and the discussion of their implications. With ethnomusicology comes the recognition of, and salute to, music as a process -- an activity of human beings.

Since music is an activity of human beings which is studied by human beings, there remains at least one further important assumption -- that ethnomusicologists will be ethical. There is no real way to check fully the assertions that "group A does this" or "tribe Y thinks that about music". One cannot even know, with total certainty, that the pressure to publish something does not sometimes call forth the temptation in some scholars to become fictional where facts are lacking. Nor can it be known whether one's presence at a musical performance or in any field situation alters that performance, or how one's personality affects one's interpretation.

Uncertainty in these and other related areas requires the mostly unspoken assumption that each one does his or her best to behave fairly, truthfully, objectively and ethically. Those of us who train students try to instill the highest possible standards of fair and honest procedure. Yet we know that, despite good intentions and best assumptions, temptations remain and that bias will emerge. One can only hope that basic ethics will guide behavior, and when the nature of ethical behavior in a particular situation is unclear, that human decency will prevail.

The assumption of ethical behavior is, in ethnomusicology as in other realms of human interaction, so basic that it is often left unstated. All that has been said in this book, and each other work which has been cited, relies not so much on the absolute accuracy of the authors as on their best efforts to be ethical and honest. In the final analysis, then, this assumption is fundamental to all facets of human thought.

IMPLICATIONS

As an activity of human beings, music is an integral part of culture. Its form, style, presentation, persistence, reception, and evaluation have their main locus in cultural patterning of thought. It has ties with other aspects of human behavior -- especially religion. In addition, the economics, the politics and other areas of human organization and activity are also intimately involved with musical activity.

As a result, any study of music in an ethnomusicological sense implies that music must be simply a point of departure and not an end in itself. Further, it implies the need for choices.

As a point of departure, music provides an entree to both the objective aural reality of musical sound and the subjective multi-faceted realms of human thought. Every musical situation, event, or sound stream can be viewed from several aspects. Each expresses part of an interlinking mental system within a social environment in a physical setting.

Reality is complex. If a scholar is to succeed in using music as a point of departure, it is necessary to identify those aspects of social systems, behavior, or events which form relatively autonomous regularities and interdependencies of regularities for study. The implication, here, is that if interrelated aspects are ignored, if a study is incompletely delimited, then that study leads nowhere in terms of furthering musical or human knowledge.

This, in turn, implies not only a need for care in delimiting points of focus, but also a demand for strong ethics. As is the case in other areas of the humanities and social sciences, most of the responsibility for success rests upon the researcher. This is both an implication throughout this book, and a flat statement of truth.

The authors have also intended to imply quite strongly that the study of music as culture has intrinsic value. It fleshes out the understanding of human motivations, interactions, thought processes and creativity. More importantly, this type of study involves focusing on music in order to reveal emergent culture, existential culture, essential culture.

It is likely that the questions which are arousing interest, discussion and participation at one point in time will be replaced by totally different questions at another point of time. It is also likely that approaches to the study of music will change, particularly as technology makes available more and more sophisticated and lighter equipment. It is possible that even the presentation of understanding regarding music, musicians and musical systems will change through time.

Yet, music remains. A specific musical system or style changes through time, adapts and alters itself to changing circumstances. Thought forms surrounding it may also change. Yet, music as a human creation, a human expression and a human activity will probably endure. Also, it will probably endure as an enigmatic distant beacon, drawing and driving ethnomusicologists (and others interested in its study) ever forward into its beckoning light.

The pursuit of music is a pleasurable, challenging and exciting activity. The questions it raises are difficult and momentarily impossible to answer. Yet the pursuit of answers to those questions can be a joyful one. It is our hope that this book will have transmitted at least some of the excitement, some of questions, some of the rewards of this particular pursuit.

Frankly, our intent has been an attempt to be seductive. The challenges in the pursuit of music and musical systems are great; the questions are transcendental; the rewards are elusive. But the final prospects of ethnomusicology rests not with the current practitioners, but with the future ones. We have done our best; we are doing our best; we will continue doing our best.

Will you follow us and do better?

GLOSSARY

Acculturation - modification of the ways of life of one culture through direct contact *with*, or domination *by*, another culture.

Anga - special feast occasion in Tikopia.

Aural - information perceived by the ear.

Base line - a point of reference for measurement of alteration or change in any system.

Bilo - a variety of possession in Madagascar in which an individual is either made ill by evil spirits, or is forced to dance by them.

Bormliza - Maltese short verses, sung in semi-impromptu style.

Canalization - cultural process by which general needs (e.g., for liquid) become specific preferences (e.g., for coffee).

Caveat - a warning to beware.

Cognition - the mental process or faculty by which and through which knowledge is acquired, processed, stored, or disseminated.

Context - environment or overall situation in which an event takes place.

Czimbalom - Hungarian struck zither.

Dilettant - Maltese word describing both those who perform and those who love to listen to music.

Enculturation - all forms of learning and/or acquisition of awareness of musical behavior and comprehension.

Ethnocentric - the view that one's own way of life or system of thought is best, to the extent of precluding understanding of different approaches or points of view.

Ethnography - the systematic description of ways of life, customs, or world views of human groups.

Ethnologitis - depression, dejection or irritability caused by the strain of psychological accommodation due to living in a culture other than one's own.

Ethnology - the formal or scientific study of ways of life, customs or world views of human groups.

Ethnomusicology - the study of the music either past or present, of all who participate in music as creators, as performers, or listeners of sound patterns; taking into account all factors which lead to a better understanding of this particular type of creative human behavior.

Fatt - long ballad-like, factual songs from Malta.

Feasinga - larger, daytime dance festivals given by chiefs in Tikopia.

Feuku - derisive sexual songs from Tikopia.

Fundamental - the lowest pitch or sound; also, the first harmonic.

Genre - a distinctive class, type or category of items.

Haka - Maori war dance which is shouted rhythmically.

Hira-gasy - a staged presentation of long moral stories sung by eight singers and accompanied by a small orchestra in Madagascar.

Kitteri-bis - Maltese solo guitar style.

Liturgy - the authorized, officially approved service of Christian churches, particularly the Roman Catholic Church.

Mako - Tikopian word for dance.

Manitou - spirit being, particularly in North American Indian groups.

Matavaka - canoe-bow dance done by young people in Tikopia.

Melisma - the singing of a single syllable of text to multiple pitches; as opposed to syllabic style, in which a syllable of text is sung to a single pitch.

Melograph - complex mechanical aid to transcription developed at the instigation of Charles Seeger, which will display a number of characteristics of a monophonic piece of music.

Mgodo - Chopi performance events which allow for direct insults and/or comments on the behavior of members of the community.

Mnemonic device - any device or cue designed or intended to assist or aid recall of larger bits of information.

Notation - the conventions and methods used for putting music into written form.

Occasion, musical - the point of time-space focus encompassing the perception, performance or creation of music.

Oral - spoken, rather than written.

Overtones - musical instruments do not produce pure tones, consisting of a single frequency, but composite tones, consisting of many pure tones, produced simultaneously. The lowest and loudest of these is the fundamental which is colored by a selection of harmonics above it.

Pitch - the location of a musical sound within a culturally-determined sound system; a measurable number of vibrations per second (frequency) of a sound.

Purotu - expert composer in Tikopia.

Raga - traditional Indian melodic pitch and tonal systems used to delimit essential features of improvised musical performances.

Repertoire - the stock of songs, etc., that a person or group know(s) or is prepared to perform.

Rija - a variety of minstrelsy found in Madagascar.

Salegy - trance-related case-zither in Madagascar.

Serata - any paid performance in Malta which is not for broadcast purposes.

Sfida - challenge between two Maltese musicians.

Strophe - a single unit of music within a strophic piece.

Strophic - a song in which all stanzas of the text are performed to the same music.

Tauangutu - derisive sexual songs from Tikopia.

Tegbla - final, falling phrase in improvised Maltese guitar music.

Tessitura - the general position of a vocal part, whether high or low in average pitch.

Timbre - tone color; the quality of a pitch as produced on a specific instrument or combination of instruments, as distinct from the quality of the same pitch if played on a different instrument.

Transcription - the process of converting performed music, usually recorded on tape or records, into one of the conventional written notation systems.

Triad - in Western music, one of several conventional arrangements of three pitches sounding together.

Valiba - tube zither found in Madagascar.

Vendetta - that condition in which an argument leads to total lack of social contact except for violence.

Xalata - Maltese musical occasion for the singing of folksongs on a combined picnic and ride, often in a bus or cart.

INDEX

BIBLIOGRAPHY

Abrahams, Roger
    1976   The Theoretical Boundaries of Performance. in Proceedings of a Symposium on Form in Performance, Hard-Core Ethnography. Marcia Herndon and Roger Brunyate, eds. Austin, Texas:Office of the College of Fine Arts, The University of Texas.

Ames, David W.
    1973   Igbo and Hausa Musicians: A Comparative Examination. Ethnomusicology 17(2):250-278.

Anonymous
    1954   Notes and Queries on Anthropology. British Association for the Advancement of Science. London:Routledge and Kegan Paul.

Apel, Willi, ed.
    1969   Harvard Dictionary of Music. Cambridge:Harvard University Press. (1944, first edition).

Bauman, Richard and Joel Sherzer, eds.
    1974   Explorations in the Ethnography of Speaking. New York:Cambridge University Press.

Bauman, Richard
    1976   The Theoretical Boundaries of Performance. in Proceedings of a Symposium on Form in Performance, Hard-Core Ethnography. Marcia Herndon and Roger Brunyate, eds. Austin, Texas:Office of the College of Fine Arts, The University of Texas.

Behague, Gerard
    1976   Comments, The Musical Occasion. in Proceedings of a Symposium on Form in Performance, Hard-Core Ethnography. Marcia Herndon and Roger Brunyate, eds. Austin, Texas:Office of the College of Fine Arts, The University of Texas.

Berger, Peter and Thomas Luckmann
    1966   The Social Construction of Reality. Garden City, NY:Doubleday

Bingham, W. V.
    1914   Five Years of Progress in Comparative Musical Science. Psychological Bulletin 11-421-433.

Boissevain, Jeremy F.
    1965   Saints and Fireworks: Religion and Politics in Rural Malta. (London School of Economics Monographs on Social Anthropology 30) London:The Athlone Press.
    1969   Hal-Farrug: A Village in Malta. (Case Studies in Cultural Anthropology. George and Lousie Spindler, eds.) New York:Holt, Rinehart and Winston.

Bullough, Edward
    1912   Psychical Distance as a Factor and an Aesthetic Principle. British Journal of Psychology 5:87-98.

Cachia, Pierre
    1973   A 19th Century Arab's Observation on European Music. Ethnomusicology 17(1):41-51.

Chase, Gilbert
    1958   A Dialectical Approach to Music History. Ethnomusicology 2:1-9.

Clark, Terry N.
    1968   Community Structure and Decision-Making: Comparative Analysis. San Francisco:Chandler Publishing Co.

Critchley, Macdonald and R. A. Henson, eds.
    1977   Music and the Brain. Springfield, Illinois:C. C. Thomas.

Draper, David
    1976   Mardi Gras Indians. in Proceedings of a Symposium on Form in Performance, Hard-Core Ethnography. Marcia Herndon and Roger Brunyate, eds. Austin, Texas:Office of the College of Fine Arts, The University of Texas.

Dudden, Rev. Frederick Homes
    1926   Gregory the Great. London:Longmans, Green & Co. (first ed. 1905).

Durbin, Mridula A.
    1971   Transformational Models Applied to Musical Analysis: Theoretical Possibilities. Ethnomusicology 15:353-362.

England, Nicholas M.
    1964   Symposium on Transcription and Analysis: A Hukwe Song With Musical Bow. Ethnomusicology 8(3):223-277.

Faublee, Jacque
    1954   *Les espirits de la vie a Madagascar.* Paris:*Presses universitaires de France.*

Fernea, Robert
    1976   Comments. in Proceedings of a Symposium on Form in Performance, Hard-Core Ethnography. Marcia Herndon and Roger Brunyate, eds. Austin, Texas:Office of the College of Fine Arts, The University of Texas.

Firth, Sir Raymond
    1939   Primitive Polynesian Economy. London:George Routledge & Sons, Ltd.
    1952   Field Notes Taken on the Island of Tikopia. Unpub. By permission of Sir Raymond Firth.

Fogelson, Raymond
    1971   The Cherokee Ballgame Cycle: An Ethnographer's View. Ethno-
              musicology 15(3):327-338.

Gilman, Benjamin I.
    1909   The Science of Exotic Music. Science 30:532-535.
Gladwin, Thomas and Seymour Sarason
    1953   Truk: Man in Paradise. Viking Fund Publications, #20. New
              York:Wenner Gren Foundation for Anthropological Research.
Gluckman, Max
    1963   Gossip and Scandal: Essays in Honor of Melville J. Herskovits.
              Current Anthropology 4(3):307-316.
    1964   Closed Systems and Open Minds: The Limits of Naivete in Social
              Anthropology. Chicago:Aldine Press.
    1968   Psychological, Sociological and Anthropological Explanations of
              Witchcraft and Gossip: A Clarification. Man 3(1):20-34.
Goodenough, Ward
    1957   Cultural Anthropology and Linguistics. in Report of the Seventh
              Annual Roundtable Meeting on Linguistics and Language. Paul
              Garvin, ed. Washington, D.C.:Georgetown University Press.
Gourlay, Kenneth A.
    1972   The Practice of Cueing Among the Karimojong of North-East
              Uganda. Ethnomusicology 16(2):240-247.
Halpern, Ida
    1976   On the Interpretation of Meaningless-Nonsensical Syllables in
Music of the Pacific Northwest Indians. Ethnomusicology   20(2):253-
271.
Harris, Zelig
    1951   Structural Linguistics. Chicago:University of Chicago Press.
Herndon, Marcia A.
    1971   The Cherokee Ballgame Cycle: An Ethnomusicologist's View.
              Ethnomusicology 15(3):339-352.
    1974   Analysis: The Herding of Sacred Cows? Ethnomusicology
              18:219-262.
Herndon, Marcia A. and Roger Brunyate, eds.
    1976   Proceedings of a Symposium on Form in Performance, Hard-Core
              Ethnography. Austin, Texas:Office of the College of Fine Arts,
              The University of Texas.
Herskovits, Melville J.
    1937   Life in a Haitian Village. New York:Alfred A. Knopf.
    1950   Man and His Works: The Science of Cultural Anthropology. New

York:Alfred A. Knopf.

Herzog, George
1940   Stability of Form in Traditional and Cultivated Music. Papers Read by Members of the American Musicology Society, 1938 Annual Meeting. New York:M. D. Herter Norton.

Hood, Mantle
1957   Training and Research Methods in Ethnomusicology. Ethnomusicology Newsletter 11:2-8.
1971   The Ethnomusicologist. New York:McGraw-Hill, Inc.

Ilg, B.
1909   *Maltesische Volkslieder im Urtext.* Leipzig:J.C. Hinrichs'sche Buchhandlung.

Kaeppler, Adrienne
1971   Aesthetics of Tongan Dance. Ethnomusicology 15(2):175-185.

Kay, Paul
1970   Some Theoretical Implications of Ethnographic Semantics. in Current Directions in Anthropology. Ann Fischer, ed. Anthropologist Bulletins Vol. 3, No. 3, Part 2.

King, Arden R.
1976   Comments. in Proceedings of a Symposium on Form in Performance, Hard-Core Ethnography. Marcia Herndon and Roger Brunyate, eds. Austin, Texas:Office of the College of Fine Arts, The University of Texas.
1980   Innovation, Creativity, and Performance. in Ethnography of Musical Performance. Norma McLeod and Marcia Herndon, eds. Darby, PA:Norwood Editions.

Kolinski, Mieczyslaw
1957   Ethnomusicology, Its Problems and Methods. Ethnomusicology Newsletter 10:1-7.

Kunst, Jaap
1955   Ethno-Musicology. The Hague:Martinus Nijhoff. (1950, original title "Musicologica". Amsterdam:Royal Tropical Institute.

Lamphere, Louise
1970   A New Look At Navajo Witchcraft, Gossip, and Cooperation. Paper Presented at the 69th Meeting of the AAA. San Diego, California.

Linton, Ralph
1936   The Study of Man. New York:D. Appleton-Century.

Lomax, Alan
1968   Folk Song Style and Culture: A Staff Report on Cantometrics.

Washington, D.C.:American Association for the Advancement of Science, Publication #88.

Lowie, Robert H.
    1937   The History of Ethnological Theory. New York:Holt, Rinehart and Winston.

McAllester, David P.
    1960   The Role of Music in Western Apache Culture. in Selected Papers of the Fifth International Congress of Anthropological and Ethnological Sciences. Anthony F. C. Wallace, ed.

McAloon and Mihaly Csikszentmihalyi
    1975   Chapter 6 in Beyond Boredom and Anxiety. Mihaly Csikszentmihalyi. San Francisco:Jossey-Bass.

McLeod, Norma
    1964   The Status of Musical Specialists in Madagascar. Ethnomusicology VIII:3:278-289.
    1966   Some Techniques for the Analysis of Non-Western Music. Unpublished dissertation, Northwestern University.
    1974   Ethnomusicological Research and Anthropology. Annual Review of Anthropology. B. Siegel, ed. Stanford:Stanford University Press, 3:99-115.

McLeod, Norma and Marcia Herndon
    1972   The Use of Nicknames As Evaluators of Musical Competence in Malta. Texas Working Papers in Sociolinguistics, #14. Austin: Center for Intercultural Studies in Folklore and Oral History.
    1980   The Ethnology of Musical Performance. Darby, PA:Norwood Editions.

Mead, Margaret
    1952   The Training of Historical Ethnologists in America. American Anthropologist 54:343-346.

Merriam, Alan P.
    1960   Ethnomusicology: Discussion and Definition of the Field. Ethnomusicology 4:107-114.
    1964   The Anthropology of Music. Evanston:Northwestern University Press.

Murdoch, George Peter
    1949   Social Structures. New York:The MacMillan Company.

Nadel, S. F.
    1952   Witchcraft in Four African Societies: An Essay in Comparison. American Anthropologist LIV (1952):18-79.

Needham, Rodney
    1972   Percussion and Transition. in Reader in Comparative Religion.

W. A. Lessa and Evon Z. Vogt, eds. New York:Harper & Row.

Nettl, Bruno
    1956   Music in Primitive Culture. Cambridge:Harvard University Press.

    1964   Theory and Method in Ethnomusicology. New York:The Free
            Press of Glencoe.

Osgood, Cornelius
    1951   The Koreans and Their Culture. Yale Publications in Anthro-
            pology. New York:The Roland Press.

Popper, Sir Karl R.
    1968   The Logic of Scientific Discovery (3rd ed., revised) London:
            Hutchinson (1965, 1959).

Rhodes, Willard
    1956   On the Subject of Ethnomusicology. Ethnomusicology News-
            letter 7:1-9.

Sachs, Curt
    1959   *Vergleichende Musikwissenschaft; Musik der Fremdkulturen.* 2nd
            Edition. Heidelberg:Quelle and Meyer.
    1962   The Wellsprings of Music. The Hague:Martinus Nijhoff.
    1977   The Wellsprings of Music. Jaap Kunst, ed. New York:DaCapo
            Press (reprint of 1962 ed. The Hague:Martinus Nijhoff).

Sahlins, Marshall D.
    1961   The Segmentary Lineage: An Organization of Predatory Expan-
            sion. American Anthropologist 63:322-345.

Saussure, Ferdinand de
    1908   *Melanges de linguistique.* Paris:*La societe de linguistique. Col-
            lection Linguistique #2.*
    1916   *Cours de linguistique generale.* Charles Bally and Albert Seche-
            hage, eds. Paris:Payot (tr. by Wade Baskin, London:P. Owen,
            1959, 1964).

Schneider, Marius
    1957   Primitive Music. in Ancient and Oriental Music. Egon Wellesz,
            ed. London:Oxford University Press.

Seeger, Charles
    1960   On the Moods of A Music-Logic. Journal of the American Musi-
            cological Society 13:1-3:224-261.

Singer, Milton B.
    1955   The Cultural Pattern of India. The Far Eastern Quarterly, XV:23-
            36.

Slonimsky, Nicolas
    1965   Lexicon of Musical Invective. New York:Coleman-Ross Company,
            Inc.

Smith, M. G.
1956   Segmentary Lineage Systems. Journal of the Royal Anthropological Institute, 86(2):39-80.

Speck, Frank
1909   Ethnology of the Yuchi Indians. Philadelphia:The University Museum.
1911   Ceremonial Songs of the Creek and Yuchi Indians. Philadelphia: University Museum.

Sturtevant, William C.
1964   Studies in Ethnoscience. in Transcultural Studies in Cognition. A. K. and R. G. D'Andrade, eds. American Anthropologist Vol. 66 Part 2.

Traccy, Hugh
1948   Chopi Musicians: Their Music, Poetry and Instruments. London: International African Institute (Re-issued, 1970).

Turner, Victor
1967   The Forest of Symbols. Ithaca, NY:Cornell University Press.
1969   The Ritual Process: Structure and Anti-Structure. Chicago:Aldine.

Wachsman, Klaus
1976   Comments. in Proceedings of a Symposium on Form in Performance, Hard-Core Ethnography. Marcia Herndon and Roger Brunyate, eds. Austin, Texas:Office of the College of Fine Arts, The University of Texas.

Wang, Betty
1965   Folksongs As Regulators of Politics. in The Study of Folklore. Alan Dundes, ed. Englewood Cliffs:Prentice-Hall, Inc.

Werner, Oswald and Jo Ann Fenton
1971   Method and Theory in Ethnoscience or Ethno-epistemology. in A Handbook of Method in Cultural Anthropology. R. Naroll and R. Cohen, eds. Garden City:Natural History Press.